NOT SO RANDOM THOUGHTS

NOT SO RANDOM THOUGHTS

MORDECAI M. KAPLAN

1966
THE RECONSTRUCTIONIST PRESS
NEW YORK

COPYRIGHT © 1966
JEWISH RECONSTRUCTIONIST FOUNDATION, INC.
Sponsor of The Reconstructionist Press

Library of Congress Catalog Number 66-19673

PN
6331
.K32

PRINTED IN THE UNITED STATES OF AMERICA
MARSTIN PRESS, INC., NEW YORK
438

To IRA EISENSTEIN

*Who is translating Reconstructionism
into a not-so-random movement*

CONTENTS

I. MEN AND NATIONS 1-124
   1. History 1
   2. Society 4
   3. Social Justice 19
   4. Politics 23
   5. Democracy 27
   6. Totalitarianism and Dictatorship 35
   7. War and Peace 39
   8. United Nations 45
   9. Group Relations 46
  10. Education 51
  11. Ethics 62
  12. Leadership 68
  13. Human Nature 75
  14. Wisdom and Experience 100

II. RELIGION 125-216
   1. God 125
   2. Naturalism and Supernaturalism 156

	3. Salvation	157
	4. Faith	162
	5. Philosophy	167
	6. Reason and Anti-Reason	174
	7. Mysticism	191
	8. Chosen People	195
	9. Judaism and Christianity	198
	10. Prayer	204
	11. Psychoanalysis and Religion	211
III.	ISRAEL	217-254
	1. Land and Nation	217
	2. Jewish Peoplehood	225
	3. Jewish Denominationalism	231
	4. Organic Community	236
	5. Anti-Semitism	240
	6. Jews Are Like That	246
IV.	TORAH	255-290
	1. Tradition and Change	255
	2. Biblical Interpretation	268
	3. Jewish Practice	280
	4. Jewish Education	283
	5. Family Relations	288
V.	RECONSTRUCTIONISM	291-296

INTRODUCTION

MANY OF THE "THOUGHTS," here collected and arranged according to different categories, appeared originally first as a regular column, and later as "filler," in the *Reconstructionist* magazine, in random fashion. The purpose in making them available in book form, and particularly in systematic order, along with others never before published, is to qualify somewhat the assumption underlying my previous writings: that to prescribe for creative Jewish survival it is imperative to see Judaism "integrally and whole," systematically and coherently in a kind of *more geometrico* fashion, à la Spinoza. The assumption applies, of course, to life in general. The qualification of that assumption is implied in the first of the random thoughts under the heading of *Wisdom And Experience*. It reads: "There are three kinds of thinking: Sick thinking, or pessimism; wishful thinking, or optimism; and wholesome thinking, or ifism, i.e. if we do what we should, what we need will happen."

In other words, there is no more reason to assume that no matter what happens Judaism is bound to have a creative future, than to assume that the creative future of the human race is inevitable. It all depends upon the exercise of intelligent freedom to choose the good life. There is much that is tangential, contingent and a matter of chance, and therefore in need of being reckoned with, if that freedom is to be used intelligently. There is much that is "random" in every phase of human existence, which we cannot overlook; hence there is a place for "random" thinking within systematic thinking. That calls for taking into account the many "oddities" in life, that suggest themselves in the course of our reading or noting what goes on about us.

Thus the random thought suggested by a pun, "A Conservative congregation turns Reform at the drop of a hat," should remind us that our denominational divisions are not always based on differences with regard to matters of fundamental import. Or the quip, that "the past should have a vote but not a veto," calls for further thinking as to how *much* of a vote, depending upon the extent to which the past is an integral part of our collective Jewish consciousness.

I am deeply indebted to Rabbis Ira Eisenstein and Sidney Greenberg for having edited "Random Thoughts" in such fashion as to justify the title of this book: *Not So Random Thoughts*.

M. M. K.

NOT SO RANDOM THOUGHTS

I. MEN AND NATIONS

1. *History*

If you want to put history to work you have to reconstruct it in keeping with the most recent discoveries of the past.

Under the influence of political inertia, man expects automatic progress to work for his happiness.

Under the influence of spiritual inertia, man expects Divine Grace to work for his salvation.

Under the influence of moral inertia, man expects the Dialectic of History to work for his security.

History that is not merely chronology is a series of events selected by some intellectual or emotional bias and arranged into a pattern.

"Objective history" is as self-contradictory as "formless pattern."

The meaning of history is as ambiguous as that of life itself.

History can be used to support the most malignant as well as the most benign purposes of men.

Events alone do not make history; they also have to be told. History is made through the recording of it.

We should study the history of our people—not for the purpose of learning what to boast of, but for the purpose of knowing what we are.

To know what we are is a prerequisite to knowing what we *ought* to be.

❖ ❖

Hancock Park at Los Angeles has a number of pits of oil, tar, and gas. Some years ago thousands of fossil remains of various animal species were found there, most of them now entirely extinct in that region, such as lions, camels, elephants and apes. Those animals were apparently trapped in the pits and met their death either struggling against the slime or with one another for the carcasses of the victims.

The name given to that entire chain of pits is "The Death Trap of the Ages."

Both men and empires would do well to heed the warning implied in that name.

The oil and gas pits to which they look for wealth and dominion might prove to be their death trap.

❖ ❖

The history by which we are made provides us opportunity.
The history we make depends upon our vision.

❖ ❖

When Lincoln said, "We cannot escape history," he probably meant we cannot avoid making history.

The more important meaning of that phrase is: "We cannot avoid being made by history."

❖ ❖

Why study history?

A Jew who does not know the history of his people is a disoriented human being.

❖ ❖

Historians with a nostalgia for the past usually indulge in retrospective utopianism.

❖ ❖

Every people that is alive today had to displace by violence some other people.

That original act of violence is the original sin, from the chain reaction of which mankind is still suffering.

❖ ❖

So far, no civilization has ever failed to "kick," once it gorged and "grew fat." (See Deut. 32, 15)

❖ ❖

Every human era has been one of transition, crisis, and alienation.

In every society there are some who experience "a feeling of isolation, homelessness, and insecurity."

The difference is merely in the number of people involved.

So far, human progress has consisted in the growth of that number.

❖ ❖

Each time some invention revolutionizes human life, man's world is thrown into chaos and a new world has to come into being.

With the creation of each such world, man has to begin anew the process of learning to be human.

This is why civilization's course does not run straight, but in spirals as around a mountain, returning on itself more often the higher it rises.

❖ ❖

Don't merely know history but make history.

❖ ❖

Our lives are what we make them.

Man can make something of himself. The making of man is the meaning of history.

❖ ❖

Our past is not merely to supply wants but to create wants, furnish information and supply inspiration.

An empire might be acquired in a fit of absence of mind, but it is lost through deliberate absence of heart.

2. *Society*

Law is not necessarily an instrument of justice—any more than a policeman is necessarily an instrument of law.

The wrong kind of law is superfluous.
The right kind of law succeeds in making itself superfluous.

No amount of economic verbiage can make jungle law sound like human law.

Rabbi Eleazar (a Jewish sage of the fourth century) quoted a Greek saying that "A king does not recognize a written law," and added, "but the Holy One, blessed be He, is different. When He issues a decree, He is the first to obey it."

Even laws which have teeth in them cannot be enforced, if they run counter to the general spirit of the people. Such laws are like dentures that don't fit.

Moral law operates through self-restraint.
Juridical law operates through external restraint.

When juridical law is based on moral law, the external restraint through which it operates is actually a form of collective self-restraint.

❖ ❖

"No general proposition is worth a damn," wrote the late Justice Holmes; as such we may include his own.

Humboldt stated the matter more wisely when he said: "Without serious attention to details, all generalizations are mere phantasma."

❖ ❖

For *law* to remain supreme, *laws* must be subject to change.

❖ ❖

"Let reverence for the laws," said Lincoln, "be breathed by every American mother to the lisping babe that prattles in her lap, let it be taught in the schools. . . . And in short, let it become the political religion of the nation."

Contrast that with the teaching of the Apostle Paul who said that "no law is ever made for honest people, but for the lawless and the insubordinate." (I Tim. 1, 9)

The Pharisees have been made the butt of ridicule by the disciples of Paul, both ancient and modern, on the ground that theirs was a religion which stresses obedience to law rather than a mystic faith.

By the same token, Lincoln should be denounced as a Pharisee of Pharisees, for making reverence for the laws "the political religion of the nation."

Well, Lincoln and the Jews make good company.

❖ ❖

If some of us are troubled over the fact that the Orthodox element in Israel is obstructing the modernization of Jewish law, we might draw consolation from a volume recently published in London under the title *Reform of the Law*.

The purpose of the book is to point to "the senile debility of much of the 20th century law of England—and it is nobody's business." So far no official body is charged with the duty of keeping the law up to date.

The book proposes the inclusion of a Ministry of Justice.

That was the suggestion of Jeremy Bentham, but it has not been acted on to this day.

In Israel there is a Ministry of Justice, but its function is stymied by the Rabbinate.

❖ ❖

To recognize that a law, which has been enacted after calm deliberation, with the voluntary consent of those properly qualified and authorized to enact it, is above the arbitrary mob-will of the people, is to accept the Kingdom of God.

❖ ❖

What is the difference between a progressive and a reactionary?

A progressive is like a man who tries to walk up on a descending escalator.

A reactionary is like a man who tries to walk down on an ascending escalator.

❖ ❖

Our forebears would not sit down to a meal without the ritual of washing their hands.

Our contemporaries will not sit down to dinner without strictly observing the ritual of washing their throats.

❖ ❖

If we didn't treat human beings as integers, we wouldn't make status a criterion of their value.

❖ ❖

When we compare the earnings of a popular movie star with the salary of the President of the United States, we become aware how much more eager people are to be amused than to be served.

On the other hand, the fact that, if you had the choice, you would probably prefer to be President to being an illustrious movie star, shows that you realize money values are no index of what really counts in human life.

Of what use is it to tell people who don't think, "It's later than you think"?

Formerly precocious children used to lisp poetry. Nowadays they lisp Freud.

The reason social scientists are less dependable than the weather-man in their prognosis is that they know even less about the mental climate than he does about the weather.

Do not be surprised that the poor, who are harassed by daily anxieties, are not given to appreciating the values of the mind and spirit.

Have you ever had occasion to hike, with torn shoes, on one of the dirt roads in the countryside, where sharp ledges of rock jut out every few yards, and pebbles and broken stone lie around loose in between?

You will recall how you were so busy picking your steps that you had no eyes for the wooded hills in the distance and the deep blue sky overhead.

Nor be surprised that those whose energies are spent in amassing wealth are insensitive to the values of the mind and spirit.

Have you ever sat glued to the steering wheel of a car as it races along on the highway?

You enjoy, to be sure, the sense of power as the machine responds to every move you make.

But you would not dare allow your eyes to tarry for one moment on any enchanting spot. You have to watch the road intently to avoid collision.

Noticing an ordinary housefly among the passengers in the airplane, I concluded that being able to make use of the most advanced methods of transportation is not necessarily a sign of progress.

Treat the typical German ill, and he will call you a barbarian. Treat him well, and he will say you must have a bad conscience.

Nouveaux riches are the victims of too much and too soon.

Thanks to the American penchant for belonging, every individual of us is dismembered into numerous memberships.

Thus far, society has not found a third alternative to being either atomized or automized.

We wake up every morning to learn of some new crisis.

We fall asleep every night with the cry of emergency ringing in our ears.

Formerly human life was like rowing a boat on a river within sight of land on either side.

Nowadays it is like hanging on to a raft amid ocean waves after our ship has sunk.

It is too bad that many a good cause has to waste on fireworks the powder that it needs in battle.

What happens to those of our young people who go forth into the world with great dreams and high purposes is illustrated by a passage in Thomas Wolfe's *Look Homeward Angel*, which reads as follows: "There was forever in that town a smell of tobacco, biting the nostrils with its acrid pungency. It smote the stranger, coming from the train. But within a day, the stranger could smell it no more."

❖ ❖

The U.S. Bureau of Census figures show that parents with the least mental and financial ability to raise children produce twice as many children as parents of highest intelligence and income.

And yet people wonder why, with all our improvements in the *conditions* of living, there has been no improvement in the *art* of living.

❖ ❖

Those who put their faith in technology and expect it to emancipate human life should be reminded that, if not for Eli Whitney's invention of the cotton gin in 1794, slavery would have died of itself in the South before many years were over, and the U.S. might have been spared the Civil War and the apparently insoluble Negro problem.

❖ ❖

When Charles Chaplin wanted to go in for more serious pictures, he said to Max Eastman: "As one grows older he wants to do something that will give him some spiritual satisfaction. I hate the word 'spiritual,' but you know what I mean."

There is much that is rotten in a society in which one "hates" the word "spiritual."

❖ ❖

It is about time that we stopped talking of the failure of religion, education, and civilization to improve man, and began to talk of the failure of man to improve religion, education, and civilization.

❖ ❖

Julius Caesar did not have the calendar year begin, as it logically should, on December 26 at solstice, but ten days later, in the hope that by that time his fellow-Romans would be sobered from the debaucheries of the Saturnalia.

He could not outwit, however, the hotel and resturant owners with an eye to business. All they had to do was to transfer the debaucheries to January first.

❖ ❖

There was a time when the worst that could be said to impugn the dignity of man was that he was nothing but a machine.

How far we have gotten away from that time is evidenced by the fact that human beings would be glad to be treated with as much consideration as machines.

Thus, the President's Board of Inquiry, in the hope of preventing a steel strike, once suggested a total increase of ten cents per hour for security benefits. The argument which the Board advanced was that management had the obligation to take care of "depreciation in the human machine in much the same way as provision is made for depreciation and insurance of plant and machinery."

❖ ❖

One who knows how to make money becomes a successful business man.

One who knows how other people make money becomes an expert economist.

❖ ❖

Banks operate with one of the most important spiritual forces, credit.

The only trouble is that they are entirely too materialistic about it.

They trust you most when you need them least.

When I got through reading the news about the hydrogen bomb, I became jittery; because the problem of where on earth to live was no longer merely a question of finding a suitable apartment. The whole earth has become unsafe.

But as luck would have it, all my fears were immediately allayed.

Next to the very column about the hydrogen bomb was the heartening news that the Harvard astronomers were off to South Africa for the purpose of exploring the 30 thousand light years of space between the earth and the center of the Milky Way.

Among the millions of the interstellar bodies which they study they will undoubtedly find a nice cozy little planet where it might be safe to live.

The method of the assembly line pervades our American culture from the manufacture of cars to the manufacture of opinions.

Presumably there is something unethical about advertising, or the way it is conducted, since it is unethical for doctors to advertise.

The two things we have not learned how to put into circulation: the hoards of gold stored in the vaults of Fort Knox, and the ideas stored in the great libraries of the world.

Among the "great" contributions of Western Civilization to the "benighted" millions of Asia and Africa are syphillis and the doctrine of original sin.

❖ ❖

Many a party, cause or institution that takes money "right and left" is far from being non-partisan.

❖ ❖

If you want to succeed as a prophet, prophesy evil.

❖ ❖

There would not be anything wrong with mammon, or the spirit of money, if it were not *capitalized,* or spelled with a capital "M."

All our troubles with mammon stem from our raising it to the status of a god.

The apotheosis of mammon has made it the measure of all human values.

❖ ❖

Nowadays, certain scientists affirm the theory known as "entropy," which means that the world is running down.

The ancients, more concerned with man than with the world, took for granted that man was petering out.

Our Jewish ancestors taught: If our predecessors were angels, we are mere men; and if our ancestors were mere men, we are mere asses.

Horace, speaking for the Romans said, "Our fathers, viler than our grandfathers, begot us who are even viler, and we shall bring forth a progeny still viler."

Looked at from a different angle, all these prophesies of doom reflect a divine discontent with the world and human life as it is.

This discontent may itself be a promise of better things to come, and therefore it belies the theories, both ancient and modern, of human deterioration.

❖ ❖

The road to the future lies between the Charybdis of despair which says: "Let us lie down and die," and the Scylla of abandon which says: "Let us eat and drink, for tomorrow we die."

An ancient civilization was all ends and no means.
A modern civilization is all means and no ends.

Being on the verge of universal disaster is mankind's chronic ailment.

Nazi diabolism has contaminated some of the most helpful and indispensable human values.

Munich has rendered "compromise" untouchable; Vichy has done that to "collaboration."

To permit them to remain untouchable is to refuse to exorcise the evil spirit of Nazism.

It makes one sad to see how the west winds have almost succeeded in effacing the hieroglyphics on the west side of the obelisk in Central Park. It looks like a symbolic forecast of what the spirit of the West is destined to do to the civilization of the East.

The nations are like blinded mules that circle around fixed poles to the rhythm of war, inflation, depression, war, inflation, depression.

Exchanging goods and services could, under normal circumstances, be a more civilizing influence than exchanging ideas.

It is said that between 1840-1940 the mechanical horsepower at man's disposal has increased a thousandfold. With atomic energy in the offing, it will probably have increased a million times before many years.

Human beings are emotionally as immature as in 1840.

Imagine entrusting hand grenades to a seven year old brat, who has managed to demolish a houseful of furniture with his toy hatchet.

Such is the present state of world security.

❖ ❖

It is true we are thrust into a world we did not make.

But who makes the world into which our children are thrust?

❖ ❖

The modern airplane has made reality of the myth of Icarus.

Likewise modern automation is making a reality of the myth of the Golem.

❖ ❖

The contemporary tendency to treat progress as an illusion is only a temporary aberration.

❖ ❖

Not all contemporary primitives are to found in Africa, Asia and Australia.

❖ ❖

It is amazing that our Rabbinic sages, who were nurtured on the belief in miracles, taught that "We must not rely on miracles" (*B. Pesahim* 64b).

Perhaps our "friend," Arnold Toynbee, would have been more reliable in his prognosis, if he had learned that truth from the "fossil civilization." He would then not have concluded from all his learning that only a miracle can save mankind.

As Herbert Muller, a less well known but far saner interpreter of history, puts it, "If we want to save our world, not merely our private souls, we might better try to keep and use our heads."

❖ ❖

According to the late Justice Felix Frankfurter, we will make little headway against crime until we take the drama out of it.

By the same token, we will make little headway with virtue until we *put* drama into it.

The small child is said to fluctuate constantly between feeling omnipotent and feeling annihilated.

If that is the case, then the present condition of mankind seems to be a form of infantilism.

A Presbyterian minister who writes about Billy Graham, in the *Christian Century,* describes him as "scientifically obscurantist, intellectually peurile and psychologically dangerous."

Then he tells us that Billy Graham was the guest of honor at an Oakland luncheon attended by 500 ministers, theological professors and seminary students.

And he winds up by saying: "I hope Billy Graham keeps growing—and I hope he comes back."

The American nation is in a bad way when an enlightened and intellectually mature minister thus succumbs to mob hysteria.

A far more convincing proof of man's original sin of pride than the story of the Garden of Eden is the sense of superiority and contempt with which some philosophers and scientists regard the common man.

Unlike Jeremiah, who agonized over his jeremiads, our modern Jeremiahs who bewail the times are having the time of their lives from the royalties which their jeremiads bring them.

The modern world is preoccupied with the difference between **right and left.**

The ancient world was busy pointing out the difference between above and below.

Let us hope that men will realize that life is multi-dimensional and is distorted when reduced to but one dimension.

Those who are afraid that debunking may have a demoralizing effect apparently consider morale as dependent upon bunk.

It may be all right to homogenize ordinary milk. But it won't do to homogenize the milk of human personality, and try to get everybody to think alike and act alike. But it will do to have it pasteurized from the bacteria of selfishness.

Beware of people who combine massive intellectual ignorance with brilliant powers of salesmanship.

Public relations experts work on the principle that the most important contacts are those with the subconscious.

There's nothing like unity to fight over.

The prohibition era of our country is noted for its release of many an inhibition.

It is amazing to what varying periods of history our contemporaries belong; most are pre-historic, and some are post-historic.

Surprisingly few of our contemporaries are contemporaneous.

The highly mechanized efficiency with which the fund-raisers pressure people into giving money for various causes reminds one of a skit by Charlie Chaplin.

A beggar sits at a busy intersection. People hurry by like automata. Every now and then some one is moved to hand the beggar a nickel, who receives it in the same perfunctory function it is offered, and rings it up on a cash register.

According to Lin Yutang, the Chinese are Confucianists when all goes well, and Buddhists when they are in trouble. Our Western intellectuals are atheists when all goes well and confusionists when they are in trouble.

Money is transformed by money power into horsepower.

Instead, however, of the man riding the horse, it is the horse nowadays that rides the man.

Only an impractical *melammed* (teacher) like Socrates could have argued that the State ought to subsidize him, instead of killing him, because his criticisms were directed to one end, to make men better.

Not in his day nor in ours do men want to be better.

They want to be happier.

The future of mankind will be determined not by the use we make of metaphysics but of microphysics, with the immense powers of the nucleus which it places in men's hands.

What with brainwashing as practiced by the Communists and brainwashing as practiced by the Existentialists, our grandchildren will ask: What are brains for anyhow?

The answer will probably be: They are a vestigial organ of a pre-modern phase of human development. Their presence makes itself felt when an original idea invades them, through what is known as brain fever.

The power that creates new responsibilities is never able to catch up with the need for the power to meet them.

❖ ❖

The pressure of industry for the continued manufacture of obsolete weapons belongs to the same class of vested interests as the pressure of the clergy for the continued promulgation of obsolete ideas.

❖ ❖

The more civilized man is the harder he finds it to live. The growth of civilization is growth in the number of mutually conflicting interests and in the number of choices he is called upon to make.

❖ ❖

An optimist is one who believes that this is the best of all possible worlds, and a pessimist is one who is afraid that the optimist is right. The problem is not whether it is best or worst, but how to go about making it better.

❖ ❖

Mankind has been caught in the fateful race between the augmentation of power and the ability to bring it under control. So long as the latter fails to catch up to the former, mankind is liable to become extinct.

❖ ❖

The trouble with the organization man is that he lacks *self-employment*.

❖ ❖

It will take the computer revolution to determine how much more of a revolution it is than any of the other previous revolutions.

Will it, however, be able to answer the question, "So what?"

❖ ❖

Every institution is the lengthened shadow of a man, but a university should be the lengthened shadow of a people or its civilization.

3. Social Justice

Civilization arose as soon as the human being began to sense conflict between his own claims as an individual and those of society.

❖ ❖

Social ideas that are not embodied in law are like disembodied souls. That is why they always seem spooky to those who have a vested interest in the status quo.

❖ ❖

When thought puzzles get to be as popular as word puzzles, we shall begin to solve our social riddles.

❖ ❖

The prophets' denunciations of their contemporaries make great literature.

That they had little effect when they were first uttered does not detract from their greatness.

Who would want the prophets to have joined Dale Carnegie's course in "How to Win Friends and Influence People?"

❖ ❖

Mankind has not as yet invented a social order in which it is possible both to do what we wish and get what we want.

❖ ❖

Theologians will some day have to give an accounting to God why they left it to social reformers and social psychologists to stress the sense of social responsibility.

Usually, those who fare well insist that the welfare state bodes ill.

❖ ❖

Karl Marx's greatest discovery is that the economic process tends to socialize itself.

That does not necessarily mean that it also tends to socialize the human being. All it means is that inanimate machines lead to the organization of animate machines. A socialized economic process is compatible with robotized humans.

To humanize man, the economic process has to be geared to such human purposes as human dignity, love of fellowman, and faith in God.

❖ ❖

According to Alexander Hamilton, "Every man ought to be supposed a knave, and to have no other end, in all his action, but private interests."

According to Goethe, "if we take people as they are we make them worse than they are. If we treat them as they ought to be, we help them become what they ought to be."

According to the Jewish Sages, "Regard all people as knaves, but treat them as though they were saints" (Derekh Eretz Rabbah 45).

Whose guidance shall we follow in our business ethic?

❖ ❖

The one kind of division of labor that will never work is a world half free and half slave.

❖ ❖

Of all the bridge-builders, those who succeed in throwing a bridge over the chasm between creed and deed wil be the most blessed.

❖ ❖

When prices and wages play tag with each other, wages is always "it."

❖ ❖

The abuse of any of the four freedoms destroys the other three.

❖ ❖

One has yet to hear of any quick remedy for social ills that isn't a quack remedy.

❖ ❖

Among his numerous illustrations of the Golden Mean as the ideal state, Aristotle overlooked the most important one—that between the extremes of poverty and wealth.

The Jewish Sage in *Proverbs* did think of that ideal state. He prayed that he be neither poor nor rich. He did not want riches, lest he deny God, nor poverty, lest he steal and swear falsely.

But he too forgot to pray *for society as a whole,* that it be spared the extremes of poverty and wealth.

❖ ❖

One of the most striking changes in the mentality of human beings is high-lighted by the fact that the Prophet Ezekiel found it difficult to convince his contemporaries that children should not suffer for the sins of their parents.

They thought that it was nothing more than just that children should be penalized for their parents' sins.

Apparently it is not enough to *demand* justice. It is even more important, though far more difficult, to *define* justice.

❖ ❖

To glory in the disappearance of slavery is like boasting, in the days of the automobile, that we are rid of the horse-thieves.

❖ ❖

He who hopes to make amends for violation of justice by giving charity is like an assassin who expects to go free because he paid the funeral expenses of his victim.

❖ ❖

The slogan, "Human rights are above property rights," is generally hurled by politicians as though it were a verbal bomb to blow up monopolistic interests. On examination it turns out to be a dud.

Why? Because any right whatever is a human right, property rights included.

And because no human right means anything unless it is convertible into some kind of property right.

If you can't function like a thermostat by regulating the social temperature, at least function like a thermometer by being sensitive to the changes in it.

The division of labor, according to which some have the dividends and the rest do the labor, does not work out.

The power to bargain is indispensable to human dignity.

No one can become a person without such power.

That means that every man is entitled to enough assets to obtain the wherewithal for life, liberty, and happiness.

The worth and dignity of the individual unaccompanied by a minimum of economic security is a promissory note without collateral.

In the final count we have nothing for ourselves except what we have given.

❖ ❖

A theology which is not a plan of social action is merely a way of preaching and praying. It is a menu without the dinner.

❖ ❖

Both the ancient Greeks and Hebrews discovered that things are not always what they seem.

The ancient Greeks discovered that the way a stick in the water looks is not the way it really is.

The ancient Hebrews discovered that one must not judge men by what one sees, nor decide by what one hears, but judge with righteousness.

4. *Politics*

There is as much difference in principle between Democrats and Republicans as between the "installment plan" and the "deferred payment plan," or between "an undertaker" and "a mortician."

❖ ❖

It takes thistledown to disseminate seeds and the speaker's art to disseminate the truth.

The truth, however, with most speakers is that they disseminate all thistledown and no seed.

❖ ❖

Most people glorify inertia as stability, and tumbling from one makeshift to another as conservatism.

❖ ❖

If politics were as simple as nuclear science, we should long ago have had the millenium.

A uniform or a robe of office divests one of his personality and invests him with an institution.

It reduces him who wears it to the status of exalted scare-crow, and the people who are impressed by it to the status of scared crows.

When scientists begin to function as citizens, they sometimes demonstrate their lack of scientific training in citizenship.

Neither ignoring nor appeasing, neither baiting nor debating is of any avail with fanatics. That is what makes them such a nuisance.

When people buy the newspaper with whose editorial policy they disagree, and when audiences are made up of those who differ with the speaker, the millenium will be here.

Subjects of hypnosis have been known to chew shoe leather under the impression that it is succulent beefsteak.

When we are subject to the hypnosis of big names or great numbers, we smack our lips on artistic tripe and philosophic fustian.

Any audience worth its salt uses some grains of it in listening to the chairman's introduction of the guest speaker.

The most solemn promise of a statesman is a definite maybe.

If we are to render unto God what is God's, we have to make sure that the Caesar to whom we are to render what is his is accountable to God.

This is what Jesus seems to have overlooked in his evasive reply to the Pharisees.

Yet this is precisely what Thoreau lived up to, and he was put in jail for it.

❖ ❖

In our masquerade kind of world, it would be most difficult to decide which political hypocrisy deserves the prize for wearing the most deceiving mask of idealism.

❖ ❖

Envy no man in official role:
He seldom gets to own his soul.

❖ ❖

With most people, unfortunately, argument by epithet carries more weight than argument by fact.

Hence newspapers generally report not the arguments of the debaters but the epithets which they hurl at each other.

❖ ❖

Hot words sizzle in cold print.

❖ ❖

If Thomas Nast, who exposed the Tweed Ring, had become as famous as Tweed became notorious, more politicians would be interested in emulating Nast rather than Tweed.

❖ ❖

The Southern Democrats have discovered a way of keeping the Civil War fresh: they wage it cold.

❖ ❖

Most political and economic slogans are mouth-filling but mind-emptying.

❖ ❖

If there can be honor among thieves, why not socialism among imperialists?

There is no political alchemy by which you can convert the dross of national greed into the gold of international decency.

The function of being the chief outlet for credulity has been transferred from religion to patriotism.

Of the earthworm Darwin said that it takes from the depth and brings to the surface of the soil materials needed for vegetation.

Of the politician, Graham Wallace says that he deliberately exploits the subconscious non-rational elements of the human mind.

That the earthworm performs a useful service there can be no doubt.

Whether the politician does is a moot point.

If speakers had the habit of clearing their minds as well as their throats before they began to speak, they would speak less and have more to say.

No amount of ethical and spiritual idealism can counteract or undo the mischief wrought by political incompetence, i.e. the failure to combine law with freedom, or the tendency to resort to despotism to avoid anarchy.

Hume the skeptic and Hobbes the dogmatist were Tories; Spencer the agnostic and Gladstone the believer were Liberals.

Problem: Is the lack of correlation between one's religion and one's politics good or bad?

❖ ❖

The reason political dissent has become more dangerous than religious dissent is that politics has become religion and religion politics.

5. *Democracy*

Now that Mexico is to have a sculptural group to represent the four freedoms, they are likely to take them no more seriously than we take Liberty, whose statue stands at the gate of the New World, offering hospitality to the persecuted.

All you need to do with a great truth or principle, to be exempt from living it, is to make an idol of it.

❖ ❖

Where there is no diversity there is no freedom.

❖ ❖

It is not enough to prove that communism is a devil.

We also have to demonstrate that democracy is not the deep sea.

❖ ❖

Referring to the fact that Eugene V. Debs, the greatest political saint America has produced, was clapped in jail, James Rorty adds: "Twenty-four hours in the average American jail is enough to convince any intelligent person that what we call American civilization is a gross failure, a contemptible fraud."

We accept Rorty's moral indignation but not his logic.

After all, the same civilization that produced its filthy American jails also produced Eugene V. Debs.

❖ ❖

There would have been no such thing as freedom of religion or liberty of conscience had there not been a secular state to enforce it.

That fact reveals the absurdity of the Augustinian doctrine that the state is the creation of Satan who moulded it out of man's original sin.

❖ ❖

In good days, Europeans seldom had a good word to say for America.

But now that so many must endure America's help, they have to be superhuman not to hate her.

❖ ❖

The difference between handling people and getting along with people is the difference between totalitarianism and democracy.

❖ ❖

Reinhold Niebuhr has defined democracy as "a method of finding approximate solutions for insoluble problems."

That, in our opinion, will do even better as a definition of theology.

❖ ❖

Long before the Nazis made an art of scientific faking to justify their radicalist theories, our own South had developed that art to justify slavery, and was later joined in it by the North to justify keeping out Jews and Italians.

❖ ❖

In view of the loose talk that we hear nowadays about the indebtedness of democracy to Christian tradition, it might be well to become acquainted with the actual facts of Anglo-American history.

"These historical facts make it very clear," says T. S. G. Northrop in his book, *The Meeting of East and West,* "that the Protestant Reformation and its religion by themselves do not necessarily produce democracy and its conception of religious toleration as a positive good."

Robespierre guillotined his political opponents in the name of *l'Etre Suprême* (The Supreme Being).

In combating totalitarianism, democracy must give better proof of its authenticity than lip service to religion.

The ancients were as eager as the best of us to know the truth.

What they did not realize, however, was that, to attain and maintain the truth, freedom of thought and discussion was a *sine qua non.*

What the written constitution of a people means depends upon its mental constitution.

By the same token that there are more ways than one to be human, there are more ways than one to be a Jew, a Christian, or an American.

The basic fallacy of "rugged individualism" is the one Jeremy Bentham was guilty of when he said: "No one knows what is for your interest so well as yourself."

The Passover *Haggadah* has the right idea of freedom.

Before it has anything to say about freedom, it wants to make sure that "all who are hungry" are provided for.

Government *of* the people is compatible with despotism; government *for* the people is compatible with totalitarianism. Only government *by* the people spells democracy.

The essence of democracy is not freedom. Freedom is only a prerequisite to the essence of democracy, which is *the belief that the people can and should govern themselves.*

That is a new ideal, which the ancients could not even have dreamt of, an ideal on the assumption that every normal human being is entitled to exercise some measure of power or influence as a prerogative of his very humanity.

Without some measure of inalienable power or influence, the human being cannot exercise the creative responsibility necessary to being human.

This may have motivated the first philosopher of democracy, John Locke, to identify it with the inalienable right of life, liberty, and *property*. For without the inalienable right to some minimum of property, enough to assure the human being independence of charity or the dole, he is helpless and powerless.

By substituting "the pursuit of happiness" for property, Jefferson meant well; but he drew the teeth out of the basic principles of democracy, namely, that *every* human being is entitled to enough economic independence to exercise power or influence through government.

Only then can we have "government by the people."

Judaism's native passion for true democracy is reflected in one of the most frequently repeated but seldom interpreted prayers included in "Grace After Meals":

"We beseech thee, O Lord our God, let us not be in need either of the gifts of mortals or of their loans, but only of Thy helping hand."

❖ ❖

If we will not make a frying pan out of democracy, no one will jump out of it into the fire of communism.

❖ ❖

The reactionaries, who wish to talk us out of democracy, pretend that the reason democracy makes use of majority rule is that it has faith in "the inevitable wisdom" of majorities.

That is a deliberate piece of sophistry to disparage democracy. The only reason democracy favors majority rule is a pragmatic one.

Democracy is safer in the hands of the majority than in those of the minority, however wise the latter be.

President Wilson formulated the political ideal of mankind when he spoke of making the world safe for democracy.

By the same token, the religious ideal of mankind ought to be to make the world safe for man's destiny to become fully human.

Insofar as democracy is essential to man's becoming fully human, it is a religious no less than a political ideal.

A democracy is a social order in which all people are sufficiently well off to wish to better themselves.

Not even the communists could improve on filibuster as a method of talking democracy to death.

There is evidently something protean about the feudal order of society.

Else how does it manage to establish itself in democracy, in fascism, and in communism with the same naturalness and ease as in the days when knighthood was in flower?

It is natural and just for the Anglo-Saxon spirit to be predominant in American life, but not dominant.

We have as little right to renounce our own freedom as to deprive others of their freedom.

❖ ❖

Democracy emphasizes what men are and what they have in common.

That is why it clashes with any vested interest which divides men.

❖ ❖

Freedom without opportunity is like appetite without food.

Opportunity without freedom is like food without appetite.

❖ ❖

The truth, to be sure, makes us free. But we have to be free to get at the truth.

❖ ❖

To know when numbers count and when they don't count is the secret of democracy.

❖ ❖

Zionism shamed the intellectual Jew out of the motto: "Be a human being publicly and a Jew privately."

Americanism nowadays preaches: "Be a conformist publicly and an individual privately."

❖ ❖

The presidential election of 1948, in refuting the forecast of the expert pollsters and the professional politicians, demonstrated the difference between democracy and totalitarianism.

At the same time, it magnified on a vast national scale, for the naked eye of the spirit to see, the difference between freedom of the will and a foregone conclusion.

❖ ❖

The right to be different is only the obverse of the duty to be oneself.

❖ ❖

Democratic freedom is the freedom of the public park and not of one's own back yard.

The veto principle which makes unanimity a requirement of public bodies transfers the lunatic fringe to the center of things.

Unity in diversity may only make a universe of discord, but any kind of universe is better than chaos.

We prevent a pond from becoming stagnant not by throwing pebbles to ruffle its surface, but by facilitating the outflow of its waters.

The way to prevent society from becoming stagnant is not by carping criticisms, but by creating the institutions and measures which keep its life on the move.

Democracy is as little known socially and politically as is the Antarctic geographically.

Among the first discoverers of unknown regions of the earth were pirates bent on plunder; nowadays geographic exploration is undertaken by scientists bent on knowledge.

Democracy, however, being still in its first stages, is occasionally furthered by men who are as little interested in it as were the pirates in the regions they discovered.

The late General George S. Patton was such a man, as can be seen from the following:

"Far too much fuss," he said, "has been made regarding denazification of Germany. This Nazi thing is just like a Democratic and Republican fight."

Free enterprise, when free of all social responsibility, tends to grow to a point where its predatory propensities overshoot the mark.

That is very much like what we are told about the saber-toothed tiger.

Its long canine teeth kept on growing until they became so long that the tiger could not bite effectively, and it became extinct.

❖ ❖

Liberalism is an *ism* which stresses freedom.

The trouble with liberalism is that it tells us what to be free *from,* but does not tell us what to be free *for.*

There is no "freedom *for*" even among the Four Freedoms.

❖ ❖

In the struggle for world leadership, America offers universal peace, while Russia offers universal plenty.

Man being what he is, America hasn't a ghost of a chance to win on that basis.

There is no reason why America should not stress by word as well as prove by act that democracy can bring universal plenty, as well as universal peace, based on freedom instead of slavery.

❖ ❖

We Jews have to learn to live under freedom and in a climate of diverse opinion.

That calls for an intellectual and spiritual metamorphosis on our part analogous to that which sea animals undergo when they become land animals.

Will we be able to undergo such a metamorphosis?

The answer is implied by Rachel Carson in *The Edge of the Sea,* "The tidal strip of the seashore—between the mark of the high tide and low—was the cruel training ground where the sea creatures learned to live on the hostile land."

❖ ❖

Virtue is that use and distribution of power which leaves no one powerless.

❖ ❖

It will take a long time for mankind to learn that the alternative to Savonarola's theocracy (based on the miraculous intervention of God in man's affairs) is *not* necessarily Machiavelli's cynical conception of government (the domination of the weak by the strong).

❖ ❖

Those who believe that people should be free to destroy freedom belong to the muddle-class liberals. (And that is no typographical error, either!).

❖ ❖

Freedom of thought is the essential freedom, not freedom of speech. After all, there should be some restriction on a madman's freedom of speech. One is not free to cry fire in a crowded house, not only when there is no fire but even when there is one.

❖ ❖

Other things being unequal both challenges and validates the principle of human equality.

6. *Totalitarianism and Dictatorship*

The only person a communist hates more than a capitalist is a communist who disagrees with him.

The same is true of a capitalist or any other "ist."

❖ ❖

When communism charges capitalist morality with hypocrisy, it is a case of the kettle calling the pot black.

❖ ❖

Why one is qualified to pontificate on eternal things because he admits to having lost his way in temporal things, only an ex-communist or an ex-radical knows.

❖ ❖

Dialectic, which is the process of self-correction, inherent in life and mind, will ultimately eliminate the atheism from Marxist dialectics.

❖ ❖

The main evil of authoritarianism is that it purges human life of its idealistic hopes.

❖ ❖

Totalitarian regimes, both political and religious, add insult to injury by demanding not only that you have faith in their doctrines but that you be rationally convinced of their truth.

❖ ❖

Totalitarians demand freedom *of* Democracy, in the name of *its* principles; but they deny freedom *to* Democracy in the name of *their own* principles.

❖ ❖

Why is it that as soon as men unite they build a Tower of Babel that reinforces the evil in them?

When they unite politically, the Tower of Babel is the State.

When they unite religiously, the Tower of Babel is the Church.

When they unite economically, the Tower of Babel is monopoly.

❖ ❖

Nietzsche's superman cannot exist without many an underdog to provide for him.

❖ ❖

The totalitarian conception of democracy is a form of government in which all alike surrender their rights to a dictator.

❖ ❖

Communism has given mankind a new leash on life.

❖ ❖

If democracy is to compete successfully with communism, it will not be through such means as those used by Brig. Gen. Frank Howly, the former chief administrator of the American sector of Berlin.

"In contrast to the Russian plan to teach German youth communism," he boasted, "we preferred to indoctrinate them with baseball."

What Ignazio Silone says makes much more sense: "Anyone who thinks he can wean the best and most serious-minded young people away from communism by enticing them into a well-warmed hall to play billiards starts from an extremely limited and unintelligent conception of mankind."

❖ ❖

Communism's promise of ultimate freedom after the transitional stage of class dictatorship tastes like warmed-over "pie in the sky."

❖ ❖

Communism, posing as a democracy, reminds us of the demon Ashmedai, who, for a time, not only usurped King Solomon's throne, but actually tried to pass himself off as King Solomon himself.

❖ ❖

The alibi of the liberal that you can't draw the line between freedom of expression and the freedom to throw a theatre full of people into a panic by yelling "fire!" is largely responsible for the menace of totalitarianism.

Mankind should thank God for its prophets and sages, but pray to be saved from its saviors and messiahs.

The nation that gave the world the concept *Weltschmerz* at first produced the men who felt it and then the men who caused it.

If I had to choose between the doctrine of infallibility as taught by orthodox religionists and that same doctrine as taught by totalitarian atheists, I would a thousand times prefer the former.

The infallibility upon which the orthodox insist is that of past tradition, of authorities long dead.

With the aid of interpretation, it is possible to discover even in the most iron-bound tradition a few breathing spaces of freedom.

But when the infallibility is that of authorities who are still alive, God help you if you try to interpret their dictates in your way and not in theirs.

Fuehrers and dictators are human bellwethers. They lead their followers both to the pasture and to the slaughterhouse.

A demagogue, whether he be political, clerical, or economic, is one to whom we may apply the description Jeremy Bentham gave to Sir William Blackstone, the famous English jurist:

"He makes men think they see, in order to prevent their seeing."

Freedom without equality leads to monopoly; equality without freedom leads to dictatorship. Either without the other leads to violence.

Totalitarianism or any other form of tyranny is found acceptable so long as people have not had a taste of political freedom.

7. *War and Peace*

One of the main causes of war is that we have not learned to enjoy peace.

❖ ❖

It took the Second World War finally to decide who had started the First World War.

❖ ❖

It is not only religion that has to resort to all kinds of devices to win the ear of the people.

To draw the crowd to a mass-meeting to listen to what the atom bomb had in store for us, a comedian had to be "co-starred" with a Nobel Prize chemist.

A tragedian would have been more appropriate, but that would have kept away the crowd.

❖ ❖

Few are the human hearts through which passes the middle road between intransigence and appeasement.

❖ ❖

People put as much credence in cataclysm as they do in "Utopia." That is why they are as little frightened by the threat of the one as they are persuaded by the promise of the other.

❖ ❖

An example of the machine process in roboting human beings is the "processing" of recruits for the armed forces.

❖ ❖

The greatest troublemakers in the world are extremists. But for them there might not have been religious or nationalist wars. The trouble, however, is that it takes extremists to stop extremists.

❖ ❖

With the cold war in full blast, the world is like a delayed-action bomb, and everyone a member of some unexploded bomb detachment.

❖ ❖

Why is the ambiguity between peace and war referred to as "No-Man's Land?"

Is it not actually "everyman's land?"

❖ ❖

The way to trouble the waters of international affairs is to spread oil over them.

❖ ❖

Since ants and horseflies are not likely ever to discover the formula for the atomic bomb, they are likely to outlive man by as long a time as they preceded him.

❖ ❖

The philosophers formerly were wont to prove man's superiority to animals.

Now, however, that man has to wage global war and has armies, navies and air forces, he has worked himself down to the animal, and like it "carries a heavy burden with him all the time."

❖ ❖

One of the unintended effects of universal military training is an increase in the number of those who learn the art of "soldiering."

❖ ❖

World conflagrations have a habit of starting from scraps of torn treaties and shreds of broken promises.

There is no need for disavowing any resemblance between the avowed war aims and the post-war behavior of the victorious nations as "purely coincidental."

The marvel-working Bible, that always saves the soldier's life by causing the fatal bullet to glance away from him, may cause it to ricochet to the soldier near by and kill him.

We pride ourselves on having outgrown the conception of God as punishing children for the sins of their fathers. But it does not occur to us to outgrow the sins that are certain to inflict wars on our children.

Striving to become fully human has thus far been treated as an *avocation* which only the *élite* can afford to engage in.

The atomic bomb holds out the threat that unless that striving becomes a *universal vocation,* we shall all be blown to bits.

A conflagration at night reddens the sky.

The roosters seeing it begin to crow. They mistake it for the dawn.

Whenever a world-devastating war breaks out, the incurable optimists think that it is the dawn of the millenium.

Are consequences necessarily a criterion of what's right or wrong?

There was a Chinese Emperor who decreed that no man should be condemned except on his own confession. The consequence was that torture of suspected persons, with a view to eliciting confessions, became general.

Briand and Kellogg got the principal nations of the world to sign a pact outlawing war. The consequence has been that a premium was placed on starting war without the formality of a declaration.

❖ ❖

"You can never relax in an earthquake zone," says the geologist.

"You can never relax in a warquake world," says the moralist.

❖ ❖

Having dropped the A-bomb on Hiroshima, without a previous warning to the Japanese, to convince them of its potential destructive power, seems to be developing a guilt feeling which the American people is trying to suppress.

That fact should be dealt with betimes by all the available techniques of social analysis and re-education.

Otherwise God knows what the consequences might be to all the potential scape-goats within reach, beginning with the familiar scape-goat number one. . . .

❖ ❖

The defeat of Winston Churchill at the polls immediately after the war demonstrates how much easier it is to meet the challenge of war than the challenge of peace.

❖ ❖

There can be no peace in the world so long as we have to depend economically upon the threat of war.

❖ ❖

When human beings are expendable during war and interchangeable during peace, they are on the way to becoming dehumanized.

❖ ❖

All barriers, like the sea, can become highways, if we develop effective means of transportation.

❖ ❖

The argument is often advanced that just as the world has overcome the habit of going to war to settle religious questions, so it might well find new ways of solving other disputes. But this is cold comfort.

The fact that it was always the "other disputes" that called forth war, even when men called them "religious questions." Those other disputes are of protean character. They are known as dynastic wars, religious wars, national wars, defensive wars, economic wars.

❖ ❖

The ancients assumed that the Messianic Era of universal peace would be ushered in by the cataclysmic war of Armageddon.

As matters stand at present it looks as though that era will have to be ushered in by the fear of such a war. Engender among enough people in the world fear of the mutual annihilation that a hydrogen bomb is certain to cause, and there would be an end to war.

Alfred B. Nobel, the inventor of dynamite, may prove to have been right when he declared that the increased destructiveness of the weapons would ultimately make war impossible.

Thus from the seeming hopelessness of our situation springs forth hope.

❖ ❖

Dr. Hans A. Bethe, who received the highest Government award for his contributions to the peaceful and military applications of atomic energy, said: "Peace will be the greatest discovery of our time."

Peace cannot be discovered; it has to be invented. It is a matter of inventing the kind of social and economic structure for human society in general that will remove the main causes of armed conflict.

❖ ❖

Before the atomic age, whoever had anything to say about the future of mankind always assumed there would be one. Since then whosoever has anything to say about the future of mankind, always has to add, "if there is to be any."

❖ ❖

To get mass production of ideas about God, man and the world that could promote peace, it is necessary for semantics to identify interchangeable parts in all such ideas and promulgate them on a larger scale.

❖ ❖

These are the degenerations of man:
>Agriculture begat industry.
>Industry begat commerce.
>Commerce begat luxury.
>Luxury begat necessity.
>Necessity begat invention.
>Invention begat total war.
>And total war begat world cataclysm.

❖ ❖

The ages of mankind are often described as gold, silver, bronze and iron.

The deterioration of mankind and the principal ingredient of contemporary civilization are such that we may well be said to be living in the *oil age*.

God forbid that it be followed by the ash age; the phoenix is a strange bird. It might forget to arise.

❖ ❖

Remaking the world and keeping it from destroying itself are not two different tasks; they are one and the same task.

In fact, to treat them as two different tasks is to prevent either of them from being consummated.

❖ ❖

Being opposed to wars is not like being opposed to earthquakes. It may not be possible to control the forces that cause earthquakes, but it should be possible to control the forces that cause wars.

For wars begin in the minds of men.

❖ ❖

Nothing less than the realization that war must lead to the extinction of the human race can burst the bubble of complacence and apathy.

❖ ❖

The Arab refugee problem resembles that of an ambulance which, in rushing to save the life of a patient, ran over a pedestrian who insisted on crossing against the lights.

8. *United Nations*

It is highly important to be in earnest in all our affairs. But if we lack a sense of humor and we get to be deadly in earnest about any matter, then it gets to be serious, and might end up in a shooting war.

We would therefore suggest that in addition to a room for prayer, the UN install a room for laughter, where, at the end of each session, the delegates will be expected to witness a take-off on themselves.

❖ ❖

The UN is in need of revenue.

We suggest that it get sponsors for its broadcasts and have these broadcasts accompanied by a laughmeter that would indicate which lies pontificated by the diplomats get the loudest laughs.

❖ ❖

The opening and closing of meetings of the UN General Assembly have one minute of silence dedicated to prayer and meditation.

In religion, silence seems to offer the only common universe of discourse among the nations.

❖ ❖

May the day dawn soon when the United Nations will be singular, not only grammatically.

❖ ❖

Alexander the Great was a dissolute man who could commit murder without batting an eye.

Yet he was the first to try to put into effect the idea of one world, an idea which even his teacher Aristotle, the greatest thinker who ever lived, could scarcely grasp.

As Alexander envisaged the idea, it was not even to be imposed by force. It was to be eagerly accepted by all mankind.

Which only goes to prove that the Prophets were right when they maintained that God often chooses the most unpromising material for the fulfillment of His purpose.

❖ ❖

So long as the only political alternatives are isolationism and imperialism, the UN is operating in a vacuum.

9. *Group Relations*

Every human being is both an individual and a member of a people, church or nation. "Individual" and "social" form a see-saw in which neither operates without the other.

As we raise or lower the divine potential of the individual in each of us, we correspondingly lower or raise the diabolic potential of the social.

As we raise or lower the divine potential of the social, we correspondingly lower or raise the diabolic potential of the individual.

❖ ❖

Those who specialize in philanthropy are often worried by any social change that might eliminate the market for it.

❖ ❖

According to Gunther Myrdal, the famous anthropologist, the "American Dilemma" consists of high professions and low practices, especially in the matter of our treatment of the Negroes.

Such a dilemma is not only American; it is part of the dilemma of being human.

❖ ❖

In Never-Never Land, as soon as the word gets around someone has been stricken with the small pox of race or religious hatred, the people stand in line in front of the churches and synagogues, waiting to be spiritually inoculated against it.

❖ ❖

Man has at least been conceived, though he has not yet been born.

Civilization, however, has so far not even been conceived.

❖ ❖

Collective selfishness gives men all the ardor and glow of self-sacrifice.

That is why its powers of destruction, as compared with those of individual selffishness, are like those of the atom bomb as compared with those of an ordinary bomb.

❖ ❖

The moral climate of our civilization is far from wholesome.

It takes more than average strength of character to remain morally healthy in it.

Our hope must lie in the ultimate transformation of that climate itself.

That is not as impossible as it sounds.

Even the sandstorms, known as *hamseen,* which afflict certain regions of the world, and which bring to them clouds of murderous grit, can be made to disappear.

All that is necessary is to irrigate the deserts nearby and to make them fruitful.

In time that will be done.

So, too, perhaps, the deserts of human stupidity and viciousness, which breed the sandstorms of fanaticism, greed and cruelty, will be transformed into habitable and productive areas of intelligence and good will.

❖ ❖

We shall never be able to solve the complex problems of human relations, unless individuals and groups finally learn that they have to find a way of being "somebody" without being superior to somebody else.

❖ ❖

The world owes most of its troubles to the fact that too many people with a high I. Q. have a low We Q.

❖ ❖

We would avoid most of our collisions, both interpersonal and international, if we remembered the rule: "Rely on your brakes instead of your horn."

❖ ❖

We shall have more faith in interfaith when it is translated into interworks.

❖ ❖

Being a minority is not necessarily being the lesser evil.

❖ ❖

Those who advocate restrictive covenants would probably rather go to a Jim Crow Hell than to an unrestricted Heaven.

❖ ❖

A mother, who is a volunteer worker in a nursery center where a mixed group of children of different racial and religious backgrounds are brought to play, describes the little children as free from prejudices.

She concludes her account by saying: "The trouble is that children have parents. Parents teach them to hate."

Perhaps it would be more accurate, though less witty, to say: The trouble is that the children have parents, and the parents had grandparents and teachers who taught them to dislike the unlike.

❖ ❖

The higher the ideals we profess, the baser have to be the rationalizations we invent to justify our own disregarding them.

This is the inference drawn from Gunther Myrdal's *American Dilemma:* "The American creed of human equality is so flagrantly violated that it has called forth the dogma of racial inequality."

❖ ❖

The ancient Romans regarded bridge-building as a sacred pursuit.

That is evident from the name they gave to the priest, whom they called "pontifex," which means bridge-builder.

A bridge unites those whom nature divides.

Can there be a more sacred function in life?

❖ ❖

A whole mountain of uranium cannot compare in effectiveness with an atomb bomb the size of a billiard ball.

That only goes to show how much more powerful an organized minority can be than an apathetic majority.

❖ ❖

Kindness should not be limited by consciousness of kind.

❖ ❖

Next to intolerance, nothing is so intolerable as tolerance.

❖ ❖

Societies are more like one another in their characteristics and behavior than are individuals.

Hence discrimination between one people and another is even more absurd and irrational than between one individual and another.

❖ ❖

Speaking of the good will movement, a Reform rabbi said: "Whatever our *will* with regard to interdenominational fellowship and cooperation, the results thus far have not been as good as anticipated."

That was said in 1929. His remark is still not dated.

That same rabbi suggested a good-will movement between Jew and Jew.

Unfortunately, that suggestion is also still timely.

❖ ❖

Is there no third alternative to billing and cooing at Good Will meetings than killing and booing in the great world outside?

❖ ❖

Some of our fellow Jews in the South seem to forget that, by accepting the anti-Negro prejudices of their white neighbors, they are helping to spread the evil of race hatred, which may ultimately turn both Whites and Negroes against them.

❖ ❖

If you belong to the minority you must be prepared to start far behind scratch.

❖ ❖

So far as we are aware, the drive to interfaith good-will derives more from secularism than from the faiths themselves.

❖ ❖

There are many Jews who assume that fighting anti-Semitism is enough to make them good Jews.

Likewise, there are many Christians who assume that promoting anti-Semitism is enough to make them good Christians.

10. *Education*

Scholarship without a philosophy is like a lever without a fulcrum.

Philosophy without scholarship is like a fulcrum without a lever.

❖ ❖

A generation or two ago youngsters would bandy about the following conundrum:

What is matter? Never mind.

What is mind? No matter.

How far we have come from those days may be gathered from the following definition of matter which our youngsters are expected to understand:

Matter is the way the nervous mechanism with its electro-chemistry reacts to the electro-magnetic forces that impinge on it.

❖ ❖

Glittering generalities are turned out on the assembly lines of general assemblies.

❖ ❖

Education by means of pre-fabricated ideas is propaganda.

❖ ❖

The fact that there are so many educated fools does not mean that all who are ignorant are necessarily wise.

❖ ❖

Among the Jews in early Rabbinic times, the scholars, known as *haverim* or "fellows," clashed with the illiterates, known as "amé ha-aretz" (*pagani*) or "pagans."

Among the Christians in the Middle Ages, the scholars, known as the "gown," clashed with the illiterates, known as the "town."

No people has a monopoly on intellectual snobbery, and no kind of education has so far proved immune to it.

❖ ❖

The cold war between teacher and pupil will never end, unless we remove the iron curtain of authority.

❖ ❖

The rule in modern pedagogy is: Spoil the rod and spare the child.

❖ ❖

Knowledge is only half-knowledge until it becomes know-how.

❖ ❖

If public education were anything like what it ought to be, we would venture to suggest that it be made as compulsory for adults as for children.

That does not mean that everybody should go back to school and begin getting marks, degrees and diplomas all over again.

It means that the institutions by which men live, whether political, economic, social, or religious should be required to justify themselves all the time by proving that they contribute to growth of character and happiness.

"The test of all institutions of adult life," said John Dewey, "is their effect in furthering continued education."

❖ ❖

The will to ignorance not only keeps it abysmal but also renders it dynamic.

❖ ❖

The Passover Haggadah is child-centered, family-activated, ethically motivated and God-directed. That is the Jewish philosophy of education.

❖ ❖

With regard to the fourth child "who does not know how to ask," the Haggadah instructs the parents to teach him to ask.

That is the sum and substance of education.

Its main purpose should be to teach people to ask the right questions about the world and themselves.

❖ ❖

Horace Mann could imagine only one outcome of public school education: the emptying of all prisons.

The trouble with utopians is that they have a one-track mind.

They fail to realize that when their favorite project arrives at its destination, it is sure to find a large number of tracks, to any one of which the local station-master may switch it and divert it from its original purpose.

❖ ❖

It is not the in-take but the digestion of knowledge that constitutes education.

❖ ❖

The best academic education is as far away from life as the Czerny exercises are from Beethoven.

❖ ❖

If unlearning were as easy as learning, education would not be the great risk it is.

❖ ❖

It is amazing how much ignorant people have to unlearn.

❖ ❖

A teacher learned that one of her pupils turned out to be a minister, another a thief, and a third a female murderer. She asked herself what she might have taught them that had anything to do with what they came to be.

All she could recall was that she had taught them the passing of tests and the rhyme scheme of sonnets.

❖ ❖

In the race between catastrophe and education, education is fated to play the role of the tortoise, although catastrophe is far from acting like the hare in the fable.

Catastrophe is anything but dilatory, and leaves nothing to chance to gain its ends.

❖ ❖

Such short cuts to learning as fifteen minutes a day of aimless and undirected reading among great books, or passive attendance at lectures on all kinds of subjects, are invitations to ignorance.

❖ ❖

One of the main difficulties in attempting to raise the standard of education is the fact that those whose support is essential were brought up on a sub-standard education and ascribe to it the success they have attained.

❖ ❖

Measured by the cultural difference which a college education makes in the lives of most college graduates, they might as well have bought their diplomas.

❖ ❖

Propaganda aims to influence people's *wants,* so that they come to be the same as those of the propagandists.

Conventional education aims to increase people's *knowledge,* so that it compare favorably with that of the educators.

That accounts for the virtual impotence of conventional education as a moulder of character.

The ideal education would strive to increase people's knowledge, so that they would learn to want what they really need.

❖ ❖

In our competitive civilization "ideas are weapons," and to be educated is to be armed.

❖ ❖

If we are inclined to deplore the fact that our country does not look to academicians for guidance as much as it might, let us remember what happened in Germany, where academicians were taken more seriously than anywhere else in the world.

The melancholy truth is that, despite Plato's contention, philosophers are as corruptible as priests, soldiers, lawyers, and men of business.

❖ ❖

There is something illiberal in designating as liberal those studies which have merely academic value.

There is something snobbish in passing up a contemporary thing that is beautiful for an antique that is ugly.

❖ ❖

The fact that illiteracy is a curse does not mean that literacy is necessarily a blessing.

It is the use to which literacy is put that determines whether it is a good or an evil.

❖ ❖

A noted educator described the courses given in philosophy and theology both in universities and in seminaries as dealing with people we never heard of offering solutions that we cannot understand to problems that never bothered us.

Philip Wylie, in discussing "Subjective Feudalism," makes the following comment which every June, with its commencement ceremonials, proves to be true:

"The professors and students in their black robes, under their flat black mortarboard hats, keep visibly alive, even among the so-called enlightened classes, both the spectre and the spirit of the ages of darkness against which, presumably, education above all should struggle."

"We already know so much that it is dangerous not to know more," said Dr. I. I. Rabi, the famous physicist.

To which we would add, "and it is even more dangerous not to be wise, for wisdom is the art of human fellowship."

The basic fallacy underlying present-day education is the assumption that one is born human, whereas the fact is that one has to be trained or educated to be human.

A time will come when we shall finally rid ourselves of that fallacy.

Then high schools, colleges and universities will provide courses in their curricula in subjects like self-mastery, honesty, reliability, generosity, mercy, courage, contentment, friendship, freedom from hate and prejudice, a wise sense of values, etc. They may have to reduce the requirements in higher mathematics and in ancient history.

To get a degree, it will be more important to get a passing mark in the art of being human than in making a high grade in the humanities.

Until such time all our schools of secondary and higher learning will continue to be organized as "academic filling stations," giving our young people enough "gas" to drive themselves wherever they want at breakneck speed.

❖ ❖

Expecting society to utilize the education of the young as a means of social improvement is like expecting a man to raise himself by his own bootstraps.

Yet that is the only kind of levitation by which mankind will ultimately have to be lifted out of the morass of its own fallacies and stupidities.

In the language of religion, such levitation is described as divine grace.

What divine grace can accomplish we are told by the ancient prophet Joel in the following:

"Then shall it be that I will pour out my spirit on all:
Your sons and daughters shall be inspired,
Your old men shall dream dreams,
Your young men shall see visions." (Joel 3:1)

❖ ❖

Anything that is separated from its context is like the hole of a doughnut minus the dough.

The main purpose of education should be to train the imagination to see everything within as much of its context as possible.

Hillel's precept, "Do not judge your neighbor until you are in his place," stresses the need of seeing our neighbor's life with its entire net of circumstances.

That is the most ethical use to which the imagination can be put.

How to mould the imagination into an instrument to reveal the *full* context of our neighbors' lives is the main question which should engage us.

❖ ❖

Exposure to a college or university education results in a kind of intellectual suntan, which is only skin-deep, and wears off after a year or two.

❖ ❖

If you wonder why so many of our children outgrow their brightness, read how society systematically stultifies them by placing them in the hands of underpaid and overworked teachers.

❖ ❖

Thought is so difficult that people find it easier to fight than to argue.

❖ ❖

When students are given degrees at colleges and universities, they are informed of the "privileges and immunities thereunto appertaining."

Why are they not informed then of any duties and responsibilities thereunto appertaining?

"But that's only a medieval ritual," you will say.

All the more reason for changing a ritual when it has become outdated.

❖ ❖

All civilizations abound in distorted ideas about God and man. Hence education in religion or in the human sciences is *mis*-education if it is not *re*-education.

❖ ❖

An important factor in the lack of instructors in our schools and colleges is that teachers or professors "are not accorded a high enough place in the community."

The truth is that though many a professional may not be accorded the place he deserves, a profession as such is generally accorded the place which those who pursue it have earned in it.

Medical practitioners in ancient times were slaves; until not so long ago surgeons were part-time barbers. They have come up in the world, because they made it a principle to keep abreast of theoretical reconstructions and advances pertaining to their profession.

If teachers and rabbis would likewise learn to keep abreast of the theoretical reconstructions and advances in the psychological, social, and religious sciences as these affect their respective callings, they would be granted recognition without their having to ask for it.

The most fruitful answers to our problems are those which direct us where and how to look for answers.

The secret of learning is to digest what we ingest.

It is hard to disagree with one's teachers. It is harder to disagree with one's colleagues. But hardest of all is to disagree with one's disciples.

The reason most students learn little at the schools, both lower and higher, is that most of the teachers teach to live and do not live to teach.

The ideal teacher is said to be one who succeeds in making himself dispensable. He should train the pupil or student to learn to think and to do things by himself.

Unfortunately, too many teachers prove themselves dispensable without all this effort on their part.

In their graduation speeches, university presidents have a habit of stressing the need not of more knowledge but of greater wisdom.

Unfortunately, they do not display much wisdom in contrasting wisdom with knowledge. Moreover, any hint that we have enough knowledge is itself folly.

If we lack wisdom, it is because we lack the kind of knowledge necessary to help us manage our lives properly.

If the metamorphosis of man were accepted not merely as a verbal sentiment, but as an inevitable directive to becoming fully human, the main function of education would be teaching each successive generation how to negotiate the transition from the past of mankind to its future.

When medical doctors deliver babies they cut their umbilical cords.

Educators and spiritual doctors should follow a similar procedure when they deliver the infantile mind from the womb of the past.

There are two kinds of education, the kind that gives birth to wonder and the kind that kills it.

The problem of religion in American education is hopelessly insoluble so long as the only kind of religion America will recognize is church religion, and so long as each church religion will regard every other as false and misguided.

The polishing stone of modern science is not run by hand but by mechanical power.

Those who wish to sharpen their wits against it should be careful not to press them too hard, else they are likely to be sharpened away entirely.

Why do people always blame the horse when he refuses to drink the water he is led to? The water may not be fit to drink!

Truth stands little chance of winning in the market place of ideas, since in order to get a hearing nowadays it would have to resort to the kind of advertising which doesn't go with truth.

Semantics, the science which seeks to establish the exact meanings of words, may in time save politicians from logomachy (word battles) and theologians from logolatry (word worship).

In the present emphasis on know-how and know-what, we overlook the importance of know-what-for.

Every long-range program should be translated into immediate objectives. Every immediate objective should be part of a long-range program.

The thesis of Budd Schulberg's novel, *Disenchanted,* is that "the process of growing up is one of continual disenchantment, of continually shedding the old enchantment for the new."

This is the reason so few people care to grow up.

Now that we have a Book Month, how about instituting a "Think Month?"

It is well to recall what Dooley said:

"The truth is that readin' is the next thing this side of goin' to bed f'r restin' the mind. Believe me, Hennessey, readin' is not thinkin'."

11. *Ethics*

If people in a position of leadership were expected to make a career of intellectual honesty, the millenium would be around the corner.

❖ ❖

Yom Kippur should be a trumpet call to conscience (Is. 58).

❖ ❖

The best we can do is generally much better than what we actually do.
To be troubled by that fact is to have a sense of sin.

❖ ❖

One of the greatest sources of inner conflict is between loyalty to facts and loyalty to hopes.
To yield entirely to one or the other is to invite madness.

❖ ❖

Love, hate, fear and hope grow on what they impel us to do.

❖ ❖

More people are shamed into vice than into virtue.

❖ ❖

To promise is human; to fulfill, divine.

❖ ❖

The most dangerous sinners are those with a "saving grace." Their allure is irresistible and their example is contagious.

❖ ❖

Are those who object to accepting "tainted money" for philanthropic, educational, or religious purposes guilty of the "gennetic fallacy?" Do they violate the principle that not what a thing comes *from* but what it comes *to* should count? Hardly.

❖ ❖

It is said that we cannot know ourselves before we have become strangers to ourselves.

Perhaps that is why, according to our Sages, a repentant sinner is greater than an untempted saint.

Theoretically, when we are confronted by two evils we should choose the lesser.

How does that help us when we have to choose between the frying pan and the fire?

If we subtract from our philanthropy the factors of income tax deduction, "going over the top," and the competitive urge, we are lucky if there remains one percent of real benevolence.

Aristotle's fundamental rule in ethics is known as "the golden mean." It is the mean between extremes.

Maimonides accepted that rule as the basis of Jewish ethics.

If you think it is easy to follow, try to walk in no-man's land under the crossfire from both sides.

The function of ethics should not end with giving us an uneasy conscience, nor that of religion with making us ill at ease in Zion.

Most people imagine that to have the heart in the right place means having it anywhere but in the head.

Only the well-to-do can afford the exquisitely simple dress. Only those who abound in goodness can afford the exquisitely simple life.

The reluctance to face realities is a far greater ethical sin than the refusal to believe in miracles could ever have been a religious sin.

❖ ❖

When clergymen find it necessary to formulate a code of professional ethics, do they not thereby confess that the religion they profess is not of itself sufficient to make them ethical?

❖ ❖

If "making good" coincided with being good, the millenium would be around the corner.

❖ ❖

The Ten Commandments can as little be violated with impunity as the multiplication table.

❖ ❖

Man-made evil will exist as long as the imponderables will carry less weight than the ponderables.

❖ ❖

Ibsen's Peer Gynt, who acts on the principle "To thyself be sufficient," is not only an individual. He is often a family, a nation, or a religious group.

❖ ❖

A kind word is a good deed.

❖ ❖

The pleasant, the profitable, and the prudent are the three peas in the pod of selfishness.

❖ ❖

Thoughtlessness can be as cruel as heartlessness.

❖ ❖

When occasion arises for you to swallow your ego, don't swallow it whole. You may choke on it. Be sure to dissolve it first in the milk of human kindness.

❖ ❖

Spirituality is not merely a volatile form of moral goodness.

❖ ❖

Specialization is not confined to the arts and sciences.

There is specialization also in the domain of the spiritual. An outstanding example was Rabbi Israel of Radun. He specialized in the theory and practice of refraining from gossip.

❖ ❖

Other things being equal, it takes more courage to say "no" than to say "yes."

❖ ❖

To be able to distinguish between a greater and a lesser evil is the beginning of goodness.

❖ ❖

You are as likely to preach people into goodness as to start a car by saying "Giddap."

❖ ❖

The term "moral holiday" is an euphemism for an immoral one.

❖ ❖

Any cause means to a person as much as all he gives to it divided by what he *can* give to it.

❖ ❖

It takes self-consciousness to foster self-forgetfulness.

❖ ❖

How far psychology is from helping us in our human relations may be inferred from the fact that great as he was as a psychologist, Freud was not a good judge of people.

Alexander Pope seems to have adjudged forgiveness as divine, so as to be exempt from practicing it.

❖ ❖

To be fully alive we must have a mission.
But we can have a mission without engaging in a crusade.
To be militant we do not have to be belligerent.

❖ ❖

We may question the historical claim of *Torah min hashamayim* (Torah supernaturally revealed from heaven), but we cannot question the ethical duty of *Torah l'shem shamayim* (Torah for the sake of heaven).

❖ ❖

To be morally bankrupt is to be without moral assets, without belief in the existential reality of moral values.
From being morally bankrupt to being morally corrupt is but one step.

❖ ❖

We know what is unethical, but we don't know what is ethical, because there is more than one alternative to what is unethical.
Many a situation in human life is a Gordian knot which only one endowed with moral courage can cut with the sharp sword of conviction.
But using the sword of conviction to cut the Gordian knot of ethical problems is not necessarily an evidence of moral courage. A far better evidence would be the patience to disentangle the knot.

❖ ❖

Women who engage in gossip are beating their rugs from their balconies in a common yard and taking in each other's dust.

❖ ❖

Public relations are seldom, if ever, engaged in, unless they become some people's private concern.

❖ ❖

It is with justifiable pride that Jews point to the fact that the Hebrew term *Zedaḳah,* which means righteousness, is applied to the giving of charity.

But is there not the danger that righteousness itself might come to be regarded as no more imperative than charity?

❖ ❖

What does it mean to be good?

It means to make things and people better.

If you make a sincere effort to be good, people will assume you are better than you are.

If you have a tendency to be bad, people will assume you are worse than you are.

❖ ❖

"To thine own self be true, for then it follows as the night the day that thou canst not be false to any man."

On reflection, however, this should read:

> If to thine own self thou wouldst be true
> It follows as the night the day
> That thou darest not be false to any man.

❖ ❖

Ethics represents man's efforts to make over the world on the basis of knowledge of it and in accordance with his wishes and purposes.

❖ ❖

It takes more than an ethical philosophy or religion to get one to behave ethically. That does not make either the one or the other indispensable.

❖ ❖

The cosmic law of polarity implies that human beings should function both as means and as ends, and therefore learn to be both useful and wise.

❖ ❖

The main problem in the education of the conscience is how to change society without being at war with it. The only way to do that in the process of changing society is by changing yourself into what you want others to be.

12. *Leadership*

In his book *Man's Freedom,* Professor Paul Weiss says that "society needs both routine men and flexible ones."

We can count on the flexible ones to recognize the need for routine men.

The routine men, however, wouldn't be true to character if they recognized the need for flexible ones.

❖ ❖

What shall a preacher do?

If he talks generalities, he is ineffective.

If he talks particularities, he is generally the only one to feel the effects.

❖ ❖

The goal of a good teacher, we are told, should be to render himself superfluous.

But who wants to be superfluous?

❖ ❖

The best part of counseling is listening.

❖ ❖

The successful politician is one who has learned from Shakespeare's Marc Anthony that people want to be bewitched rather than persuaded.

❖ ❖

The Lost Pathfinder is the name of a book—but also an apt description of many a spiritual leader.

❖ ❖

Elder statesmen wish to perpetuate the past; prophetic statesmen wish to provide for the future.

❖ ❖

"To save a nation's soil," says William Vogt in his *Road to Survival*, "start with the hilltop and not the river bottom."

The same principle applies to saving a nation's soul. Start with the men on top.

❖ ❖

Advice to the fishers of men:
> Let your bait be an interesting subject.
> Let your line be a believable philosophy.
> Let your hook be a workable application.
> Let your sinker be a striking illustration.

❖ ❖

The demagogue compounds the fears and the baser passions of people. The selfless leader compounds their hopes and generous impulses.

❖ ❖

The trouble with the rabbinate is that the laymen expect the rabbis to be not spokesmen but salesmen.

❖ ❖

It must be that statesmen have a vested interest in international quarrels; otherwise, why should they be so adept in exacerbating them?

❖ ❖

There are those who are great because of what they do for others, and there are those who are great because of what others do because of them.

❖ ❖

It is better merely to express public opinion than to lead it in the wrong direction.

❖ ❖

There is nothing wrong with nations, churches and people that good leaders can't correct.

❖ ❖

The fact that the Lippmans, the Ropers and the Gallups have been proven wrong does not mean that the longshoremen, the charwomen and the delivery boys are necessarily right.

❖ ❖

Misguided leaders are a far greater menace than guided missiles.

❖ ❖

The trouble with most preaching is that it is as specific as the advice that in order to avoid poverty people should have money.

❖ ❖

The trouble with preaching is that it indulges in generalities that cover a multitude of sins.

❖ ❖

A good rule in preaching: strike hard and get away fast.

❖ ❖

A true leader must be more than a "sandwichman" for some popular cause.

❖ ❖

The true prophet can be described no more accurately than by using Chesterton's statement on Swift:

"He hated his perverse generation enough to want to change it, and yet he loved it enough to think it worth changing."

❖ ❖

Those who make a calling of persuading people to do what they should are condemned to lifetime enthusiasm.

❖ ❖

An ideal relationship between rabbi and congregation is one in which it can be said of the rabbi, "Light dawns for the Zaddik," and in which it can be said of the congregation, "and joy for those who are upright in heart."

❖ ❖

Where there is little inspiration there is little aspiration.

❖ ❖

"Fools rush in where angels fear to tread."

Who's to blame if not the angels for fearing to tread where they should?

❖ ❖

A visionary is a person who assumes that people want what they need.

❖ ❖

The problem of the modern rabbi is how to be a public and a private figure at the same time.

❖ ❖

There are two kinds of clergymen—whether they be rabbis, priests or ministers: philosopher-clergymen and politician-clergymen.

You can tell a philosopher-clergyman by the way he seldom remembers your name, no matter how intimately he knows you.

You can tell a politician-clergyman by the way he hellos you, slaps you on the back and calls you by your first name, though he may have seen you only once years ago.

❖ ❖

Society expects its spiritual leaders to teach the truth and nothing but the truth, but it forbids them to teach the whole truth.

Then it denounces them for teaching only half-truth, which is said to be worse than a whole lie.

❖ ❖

The trouble with prophets is that they forget one thing: you can't teach people whom you denounce.

❖ ❖

The trouble with most preachers is that there is no bite to their bark.

❖ ❖

The sum of all teaching is that the essence of all knowledge is the awareness of our ignorance.

❖ ❖

Many rabbis imagine they are in the position of the doctor whom the sick man ordered never to tell him the truth in case he should be seriously ill.

❖ ❖

The great religious geniuses of the past discovered divinity.

Those of the later generations have explored divinity.

There is no inherent difference between the two types of greatness.

If the discoverer seems greater than the explorer, it is only because the discoverer starts with nothing, while the explorer has something to begin with.

Both, however, are equally creative.

❖ ❖

The "prophetic" function of the ministry is all too often regarded as similar to that of the weather prophet: to register, but not to change the climate of opinion.

❖ ❖

If religious leaders would be as unashamed to confess ignorance as scientific leaders, religion would enjoy as much prestige as science.

❖ ❖

The trouble with many preachers is that it is difficult to make out whether what they advocate is what they themselves believe or what they want their hearers to believe.

❖ ❖

Altogether too much preaching is the art of circumlocution applied to religion.

❖ ❖

"They (the students of Newton Seminary) learned enough modern theology and historical criticism of the Bible in the seminary to pass their examinations and to get their degrees. They were too canny to preach it in their pulpits and thereby endanger their livelihoods." (*The Preacher and I*, by Charles F. Potter).

And still we wonder why religion is ethically ineffective!

❖ ❖

The rabbi as pastor deems it his duty to comfort the afflicted.

The rabbi as preacher deems it his duty to afflict the comfortable.

❖ ❖

The rabbi expects his congregants to run their businesses like a synagogue, and the congregants expect their rabbi to run the synagogue like a business.

❖ ❖

"A physician who cannot identify himself with his patients' suffering," we are told, "cannot be a true physician to his patient."

That is why a teacher of medicine said he wished he could prescribe a course of illness for every medical student.

The same is true of the rabbi who wants to be a true physician of the soul.

Unless he can put himself mentally in the place of those who are troubled by doubts or who have yielded to temptation, he can be of little help to those who need spiritual healing.

We would not suggest a course in yielding to temptation; but a course in doubting while still in his teens is actually a good thing for the rabbi.

❖ ❖

The late Stephen S. Wise, in his autobiography, in discussing the controversy that raged around his denunciation of the U.S. Steel Corporation for its fight against the unionization of its workers, mentions the fact that some ministers of religion took issue with him.

They maintained that officers of the church "should be the governing body to decide on all public utterances of the pastors."

Apparently Wise believed that ministers lived *for* religion, whereas they believed that ministers lived *off* religion.

❖ ❖

The war of a prophet with his society is a lover's war.

❖ ❖

Countries that lack high mountains, which collect the necessary water sources for the fields in the valleys, are bound to be deficient in productivity.

Peoples that lack great personalities, who might embody in themselves the necessary experiences and abilities to guide and inspire the masses, are bound to be deficient in creativity.

❖ ❖

There is a Rabbinic saying to the effect that "greater than Rabbi is the title 'Rabban,' and a greater title than 'Rabban' is the name itself."

In other words: conventionally great are they whose greatness is that of status or position, while the truly great are those whose greatness does not depend upon conventions or titles.

❖ ❖

Preachers often speak nobly and do little.

❖ ❖

There seem to have been three kinds of prophets: false prophets, visionaries and ifists. The false prophets approved of the status quo; the visionaries reveled in the glories of the end of time; the ifists were concerned with the present and sought to improve it by declaring that the outcome depended upon their contemporaries. Those ifists were the only true prophets.

13. *Human Nature*

The man no one knows: Man.

❖ ❖

Our own nature dictates our philosophy of human nature.

❖ ❖

No one can misunderstand us as much as we do ourselves. That applies to peoples as well as to individuals.

❖ ❖

To know ourselves we have to know our neighbor.
To know our neighbor we have to know ourselves.

❖ ❖

Not only of Russia, but of the human mind in general, may it be said, to use the expression of Winston Churchill, that "it is a riddle wrapped in a mystery inside an enigma."

The one thing certain about human nature is that it is unpredictable.

❖ ❖

It is only when we try to remake anything that we really come to know it.

That applies to people, as well as to the conditions under which they live.

❖ ❖

Human life looks as little like what one reads about it in the books by which one is revolted, as it does like what one reads about it in the books by which one is uplifted.

❖ ❖

Mankind marches not abreast but in long sequence. We always have with us not only pre-moderns but also primitives.

❖ ❖

Human nature, as conceived by the scientists, is as much like what human nature actually is as a skeleton of a human being is like a human being.

❖ ❖

To say a human being is merely the product of heredity and environment is as untrue as to say that a painting is the product of paints and technique.

❖ ❖

To know what his face is like, a man must depend on a mirror. To know what his character is like, a man must depend on the opinions others have of him.

But it is easier to find a mirror that does not distort one's physical appearance than it is to find people who give a true reflection of one's character.

❖ ❖

Like everything else in the world, human nature is neither what it is nor what it can be; it is both.

❖ ❖

Some people suffer from intellectual frostbite, others from emotional sunstroke.

❖ ❖

The actual human being is little more than a caricature of Man.

❖ ❖

All of men's inalienable rights are tantamount to their resposibility to make full use of their abilities.

❖ ❖

Civilization with its good and evil is as much a part of human nature as the shell is of the oyster.

❖ ❖

Mechanical brains can answer questions more efficiently and correctly than human brains, but it takes human brains to *ask* the right questions.

❖ ❖

Intellectuals are no less eager to be stroked than ordinary men. That is why they, too, arch and purr and rub against the knees of their bosses.

❖ ❖

There are three kinds of people: yes-men, no-men and but-men. The first are boring, the second provoking, the third provocative.

❖ ❖

Intolerant people are those who cannot bear to see in others the failings which they refuse to see in themselves.

❖ ❖

Being ready to resign from the human race is mistakenly regarded as a sufficient qualification for membership in some higher race, if there be such.

❖ ❖

Viewed scientifically, a human being is a machine to convert matter into energy.

Viewed commercially, a hog is a machine to convert wheat into meat, and a human being is a hog to boost the price of both.

❖ ❖

One of the main problems of human nature is how to learn to appreciate a good *before* being deprived of it, as well as *after*.

❖ ❖

Man's growth in power over nature so far has meant a decline in his power over himself.

❖ ❖

The trouble with most of us is that we try to invent ourselves before we have fully discovered ourselves.

❖ ❖

For every increase in the horsepower of drive we need a corresponding increase in the brain power of control.

❖ ❖

The ideals which determine our ideas about life are the resultant of our tradition, our surroundings, and our desires.

❖ ❖

If we don't know what we want, we are likely to get what we don't want.

❖ ❖

From the way some people act, it seems that man uses the divine image merely as a mask to disguise the beast in him.

❖ ❖

Whenever you feel like agreeing with F. G. Schiller in his *Tantalus* that humanity is still yahoomanity, bear in mind:

First, that in spite of all that vicious religion and politics have done to corrupt human nature, it still retains the power of regeneration.

Second, that no genuine all-out attempt to improve human nature has ever been made. Every system of religion, law or ethics which has thus far played a part in the world has been vitiated by some requirement, besides that of being human, for admission to its benefits.

❖ ❖

The solution of the sphinx's riddle is *not* that its human head is a mere illusion and that only its lion's paws are real.

❖ ❖

When we hope for the best and are prepared for the worst, we find life is not so bad.

❖ ❖

Both men and nations have to learn that the alternative to delusions of grandeur is not necessarily delusions of worthlessness, but a sense of reality.

❖ ❖

We betray what we are every time we say anything about someone else.

❖ ❖

Nietzsche had the right idea when he urged that man must evolve into a higher type of being.

But in urging man to become *superman,* Nietzsche forgot that man still had a long way to go to become *human.* The human race is still in its infancy.

That is good to remember when we read the newspapers. It will prevent our blood pressure from rising.

❖ ❖

What we expect of human beings is generally in inverse ratio to the amount of our experience with them.

When you are on the point of losing faith in mankind, think of the following:

1. I am disgusted with the evil and corruption I see about me.
2. Since I react that way, I myself cannot be entirely bad.
3. Let me concentrate on the good that I myself possess.
4. That should lead me to have some faith at least in myself.
5. But I am an average person, no different from most people.
6. They, too, most likely have some good in them.
7. By concentrating on the good in them, I am bound to develop at least some faith in most people.

To see life properly we need bifocals—the distance lenses for searching its possibilities, the reading lenses for noting its realities.

It is a source of common complaint that the social sciences are far behind the technical sciences in point of facts known and inferences drawn.

The reason for that should not be hard to understand.

To make headway in the technical sciences you have to know only what the most clever people have thought.

To make progress in the human sciences, you have to know also what the fools think—and there are so many fools!

Man's significance seemed to have been deflated for all time when the astronomers discovered the earth's centrality to be an illusion.

Yet at that very time his significance grew; for just then the philosophers began to discover that all reality, including the farthest reaches of man's telescope is, in a sense, the product of his own mind.

Man's moral responsibility, similarly, seemed to suffer eclipse when the biologists discovered the determining influence of heredity and environment. Yet at that time it began to shine anew, for the physicists then began to point the way to the inexhaustible sources of power by means of which he might bring both heredity and environment under control.

❖ ❖

Some of the ways of nature have to undergo considerable adaptation before they can be introduced into the moral and spiritual world. But some of its ways are in need of being made part of that world just as they are, without the slightest change.

Take an example from our own physiology:

Each cell, each organ of the human body, not only keeps itself alive, but also keeps the rest of the body alive.

If that procedure extended to humanity as a whole, what a world this would be!

❖ ❖

We must have indomitable faith in human nature, if we are not to be embittered by its savageries.

❖ ❖

The first human being who thought before he acted was the first theorist.

❖ ❖

Without imagination you can't understand your dog or horse, much less your fellowman, and least of all yourself.

❖ ❖

Many a strong back hides a weak backbone.

❖ ❖

The Ego and the Id got into a hot debate,
The Ego snubbed the Id and said: "Now you don't rate."
Temptation to retort in kind who could resist?
The Id replied in haste, "Since when do you exist?"

The one thing that biologists fail to understand is that, in becoming human, man has transferred his venue from that of the animal.

To forget a wrong one has suffered is quite impossible; to forgive is humane; to refrain from blame is divine.

The human being left to the automatism of nature would be little more than a beast. That does not mean, however, that, subjected to man-made automatism, he would be little less than an angel. All he would then amount to would be just a machine.

To know human nature as it is, the scientific approach is sufficient.

To know human nature as it ought to be we need also the ethical approach.

To be sure that it can be what it ought to be we need, in addition, the religious approach.

To describe a human being as consisting of a body and a soul is like describing milk as a combination of whey and curd.

The Kinsey Report on *The Sexual Behavior of the Human Male* treats the male population statistically, as though they had no more social and spiritual involvement than tomcats.

The fact is that "the human male" is no more true to life than "the economic man."

❖ ❖

It is just as much part of human nature to be self-spending as to be self-saving, to be altruistic as to be egoistic.

❖ ❖

Human life cannot be like a single thread. It is either, as in most cases, like a tangled skein, or as in rare cases, like a well-designed tapestry.

❖ ❖

The human mind can be impelled not only by compulsive fears and anxieties, but also by propulsive hopes and assurances.

❖ ❖

Those who promise too much and too soon often accomplish too little and too late.

❖ ❖

Human beings are the only creatures of circumstances that are also creators of circumstances.

❖ ❖

In what we are and do, proportion counts as much as ingredients. Two people may have the same ingredients of character, yet be different from each other as water and peroxide of hydrogen, which are composed of the same chemical elements but in different proportions.

❖ ❖

It is a sign of maturity to refuse to live with unsolved problems, to consent to live with insoluble problems, and to be able to distinguish between the two.

❖ ❖

A sure sign of immaturity is impatience.

❖ ❖

Making up one's mind is like making one's bed, for we generally let other people do it for us; and, further, as we make it up so we lie in it.

Alexander Woolcott's description of Heywood Broun as looking like an unmade bed applies to most minds.

❖ ❖

It is evident that a man deserves no special credit either for his natural endowments or for his opportunities.

"But," you will say, "does he not deserve credit for taking advantage of his opportunities?"

Is not, however, the capacity to take advantage itself part of his natural endowment?

❖ ❖

If our lives are fated to be like prairies, without elevation, let them at least be without pits and declivities.

❖ ❖

Love and hate sharpen the powers of observation but dull the edge of judgment.

Detachment keeps the edge of judgment keen but dulls the powers of observation.

❖ ❖

It is easier to be like our neighbor than to like our neighbor.

It is easier to like ourselves than to be ourselves.

❖ ❖

The inherent potency of man's freedom of the will, as compared with that of his heredity and environment, may be no more than that of a spark, as compared with that of a powder magazine.

❖ ❖

As long as we have rules against smoking in the vicinity of a powder magazine, we believe in human responsibility, whether or not we admit it in theory.

❖ ❖

When man discovers that the same cause can result simultaneously in two contradictory effects, he rediscovers the freedom of the human will.

❖ ❖

One of the most convincing proofs of man's inner freedom and his responsibility for what he does, is the psychological insight of Konrad Heiden that "in the long run only those can be coerced who really want to be."

❖ ❖

There can be no self-mastery without self-evaluation.

❖ ❖

An important person to be on good terms with is yourself.

❖ ❖

Doing the hardest thing first is the best argument for faith in yourself.

❖ ❖

We should cultivate the habit of not being the slaves of habit.

❖ ❖

Habit is man's second nature. A twice-born person is one whose second nature is an improvement on his first.

❖ ❖

Intelligence is often nothing more than doing knowingly in a difficult situation what an animal does instinctively.

❖ ❖

The will to live is animal; the will to let live is human; the will to help live is divine.

❖ ❖

To want is misery; to be wanted is happiness.

❖ ❖

None feel so insecure as those to whom being safe is the most important thing in the world.

❖ ❖

Newborn infants, some one said, are the last word in selfishness.

Would that it were the last word and not merely the first.

❖ ❖

People who are in love only with themselves are never objects of jealousy.

❖ ❖

A cartoon in *The New Yorker* shows an irate man sitting at his office desk with many telephones on it. "Damn it, operator," he cries out, "I keep getting myself!"

That's what happens when the lines of sympathy connecting us with our fellowmen are out of order.

❖ ❖

Self-seekers are not given to self-searching.

❖ ❖

Selfish people are ever busy running away from themselves.

They refuse to pay attention to anything or anybody that might stop them; they are afraid their selves might catch up with them and call them to account.

❖ ❖

A good way of taking a vacation is to get away for a while—from oneself.

❖ ❖

When we want to free ourselves of all responsibility, we so disguise ourselves that we no longer know who we are.

❖ ❖

Pleasure yields diminishing returns.

Happiness yields increasing returns.

❖ ❖

Being a fishy-eyed reactionary is not the only alternative to being a starry-eyed visionary.

❖ ❖

To assume with the scientific economists that to the individual cash incentive is the most potent factor in human life, is to believe that man has the soul of a cash register.

When we indulge in self-pity we rob the poor and the suffering of that which is theirs by right and waste it on ourselves, to whom it does more harm than good.

It is much harder to be right than to be consistent.

If faith does not always create its object, fear certainly does. ("History teaches that the fear of war is in itself a cause of war.")

To be "on principle" either a yes-man or a no-sayer is to be without principle.

To yield its best, the soul needs properly measured tension, as the violin, to yield harmony, needs properly tightened strings.

Like a log to a dying fire is an encouraging word to a sinking spirit.

Our real nature comes to the surface when we are anonymous, and when we are part of a crowd.

The demonic furies in the human soul need the courage of numbers provided by mobs to wreak their worst.

One has to be either a saint or a sinner to have a "passion for anonymity."

Without tension there is no energy.

❖ ❖

Surplus energy—the energy left over from the struggle for existence—if not utilized, begets boredom.

To escape boredom men either create or destroy.

❖ ❖

Character is a text which neither joys nor sorrows can correct. They only underline it, making the egoist more egoistic and the altruist more altruistic.

❖ ❖

To feel that we are wanted augments our vanity.

To feel that we are needed increases our self-respect.

❖ ❖

Not to be accepted is painful; to be taken for granted is deadening.

❖ ❖

Hypocrisy is the occupational disease of trying to be human.

❖ ❖

Condoning evil in others may be saintly when prompted by one's own potential guilt. But it is questionable when prompted by one's own actual guilt.

❖ ❖

Every truth consists of two half-truths.

A skeptic chooses neither, a fanatic one, and an idealist both.

❖ ❖

There is as much snobbishness and caste pride in a prison as in a palace, in a cemetery as in a church or synagogue, and as much under communism as under capitalism.

❖ ❖

People who never live down some extraordinary achievement seldom live up to their promise.

❖ ❖

Some new evil follows a new good, just as weeds follow the plow that breaks up the soil.

❖ ❖

We need peace of mind as we need sleep—no less and no more than sleep.

❖ ❖

If a man is to have his innate dignity and be treated as an end in himself, he must have work which will enable him to be a means to something worthwhile.

❖ ❖

You can achieve the impossible only by attempting the possible.

❖ ❖

Self-pity does not go with self-respect.

❖ ❖

Despite the assumed interaction between body and mind, no one who merely dreams that he is basking in the sun wakes up tanned.

❖ ❖

Only those who know when they are licked are licked.

❖ ❖

One of the unchangeable laws of human nature seems to be the attitude of and to the mother-in-law.

❖ ❖

Man is very different from what he was when he ceased to be an ape, and from what he will be when he becomes fully human.

❖ ❖

Freud's analysis of the human soul is about as true as a gardener's view of a rose in terms of the fertilizer that goes into it.

❖ ❖

All animals except man either find a living or perish.

Man is the only animal that makes a living.

❖ ❖

The better we know people the less we expect of them and the more we hope from them.

❖ ❖

Good will can be exercised on three levels:

On the lowest level, when it is based on good nature.

On the middle level, when it is based on principle.

On the highest level, when good nature is made into a principle.

❖ ❖

When that which is suits us, we assume that it ought to be.

When that which ought to be displeases us, we consider it a mirage.

❖ ❖

In the eighteenth century "a man of parts" was a whole man; in the twentieth he is a fractional man.

❖ ❖

Until recently "In God We Trust" appeared only on hard coin, not on paper money. Was it because we only trusted in God when we didn't have to trust in man?

❖ ❖

Being wretched with the old and miserable with the new is a universal dilemma.

❖ ❖

It takes two to make one of them a hypocrite.

❖ ❖

"Modern man is obsolete," said Norman Cousins after Hiroshima.

The events since seem to have proved that obsolete man has become quite modern.

❖ ❖

The main reason for the lag in the human sciences as compared with the physical sciences is that the scientists are only human.

❖ ❖

Human beings have two sets of values: public, which they profess; and personal, which they practice.
Seldom do the two sets of values coincide.
This is the basic dilemma of human life.

❖ ❖

To make a virtue of necessity is a common human trait.
But to make a virtue of incapacity is a distinctively English trait.
Who but an Englishman would take pride, as Lord Shelbourne did, in what he described as the Englishman's "glorious incapacity for clear thought?"

❖ ❖

In theology, when we say, "God knows," we cover up our ignorance.

❖ ❖

When man exalts his human ambitions to divine absolutes, he becomes demonic.

❖ ❖

Three indivisibles which elude man when he tries to divide them are God, humanity and one's personality.

❖ ❖

Are the evils of civilization due to the malice of human nature, or is malice of human nature due to the evils of civilization?
We shall be able to answer that question when we know which came first, the chicken or the egg.

Our overt wants are for security, sustenance, mating, power.

Our latent needs—wants we *should* experience—are for freedom, responsibility, love.

❖ ❖

Nature, whether it be the outer nature of the world or the inner nature of man, is nothing but raw material to be moulded, fiery spirit to be tamed.

❖ ❖

Not knowing which should come first, to improve one's self or to improve the world, we end up by doing neither.

Actually the only way to improve the world is by improving one's self, and the only way to improve one's self is by improving the world.

❖ ❖

The one thing human nature has so far been lacking in is—humanity.

❖ ❖

After all the trouble God had taken to make man in His image, man turned out to be a failure, and so, the Bible tells us, God said, "I regret I made man."

If the purpose of the Torah is to have us imitate the ways of God, should we not learn from this readily to admit our mistakes? Yet this seems to be one of the hardest things for men to do.

❖ ❖

We have to know the ultimate goals of human life in order to know how to set our compass in trying to attain proximate goals.

❖ ❖

To have faith in human nature does not mean that we must cherish illusions concerning it.

On the contrary, only open-eyed awareness of the evil that mars human nature is what makes faith in its latent goodness and greatness necessary.

❖ ❖

We act as human beings to the extent that we are self-sustaining, self-correcting and self-fulfilling.

❖ ❖

Rousseau to the contrary notwithstanding, man cannot be compelled to be free.

❖ ❖

The fulfillment of man has to be pushed as far into the future as his origin has had to be pushed back in the past.

❖ ❖

Man is not "something which must be overcome," as Nietzsche said, but something which is yet to become.

❖ ❖

The depths of degeneracy to which man sinks oft reveal the heights of aspiration from which he falls.

❖ ❖

It is infinitely more difficult to be self-governing than to be governed by others.

❖ ❖

Possessions generally possess us more than we possess them.

❖ ❖

The will to live is not a matter of choice.

❖ ❖

The mere knowledge of how we might have avoided a tragic mistake is no guarantee that we will not repeat that mistake.

❖ ❖

No human being can live in isolation without being mad or becoming mad.

❖ ❖

It is only because man is God-driven that he strives to be fully human.

❖ ❖

One of man's greatest discoveries is that he is part of nature. One of his greatest tragedies is his forgetting that he owes this discovery to his having invented the idea of nature.

Man may be a mistake, but he is at least a self-correcting one.

The artist enables us to see in nature, both physical and human, what we are generally blind to.

The saint enables us to discover in people goodness we should never imagine they could possess.

The child-like ability to wonder at simple things implies a maturity which has outgrown the childish attitude of taking the most complex wonders for granted.

A major suspense casts out minor anxieties.

When one gets something for nothing, one is likely to do nothing about it.

When we are given the cold shoulder, we get a touch of the horror of aloneness, with its chill of death.

Too much opulence, like too much sunshine, produces dry-rot.

Alcohol makes some gay and others gloomy.
Money makes some generous and others tight-fisted.
Fame makes some humble and others arrogant.

Problems of intermarriage are created not only by differences in religion. Similar problems are created also by differences in social background, in economic status, in intellectual interests, and in types of character.

❖ ❖

Crustaceans wear their skeletons on the outside; vertebrates wear theirs on the inside; human beings sometimes keep an extra one in the closet.

❖ ❖

Why cannot psychic medicine be as successful in increasing the maturity of human beings as somatic medicine has been in increasing their longevity?

Because everybody wishes to live long, and only few wish to mature.

❖ ❖

Some people's memories are little more than intellectual junk-shops.

❖ ❖

If there is anything worse than an old fogey it is a young fogey.

❖ ❖

People often dignify their visceral reactions by calling them intuitions.

❖ ❖

There's nothing so immature as premature maturity.

❖ ❖

In magic, in advertising, in *Mein Kampf,* and in communism, it is assumed that if you repeat a lie frequently enough, everybody, including its author, will come to believe it.

❖ ❖

Some people's diction is at its best when they are engaged in contradiction.

❖ ❖

Every tool or weapon that man makes masters its maker and gives him no rest until he tests the use of the one or the strength of the other.

❖ ❖

What is so likely to escape our notice as the obvious?

❖ ❖

To Samuel Johnson, being able to kick a stone was sufficient proof that *matter* is real.

To some people, being able to kick other people is sufficient proof that *life* is real.

❖ ❖

Poor Socrates! Plato idealized him, Xenophon popularized him, Aristophanes caricatured him, and the State killed him. Was there no one in those days to do him justice?

❖ ❖

According to Bertrand Russell, solemn people are generally humbugs.

But even he would admit that solemn people at least do not humbug themselves, which is just what cynics do.

❖ ❖

In *The San Quentin Story,* Warden Clinton T. Duffy tells of a screen star who visited the famous California prison and remarked, "Why, these fellows look like regular people, not like the convicts in my prison pictures."

"They are regular people," Duffy replied, "and if you remember that you'll have a whole new perspective on crime and prisons."

"Also on regular people," we might add.

❖ ❖

When Talleyrand said that words meant to conceal ideas, he did not reckon with the ocean of words uttered by people without ideas.

When P. T. Barnum said a fool was born every minute, he did not realize that most fools are made and not born.

When Vanderbilt said "the public be damned," he avowed openly what many who say "the public be pleased" feel like saying.

❖ ❖

When Laplace was asked by Napoleon as to where God came in under his view of the world, he is said to have drawn himself up haughtily and to have replied: "Sire, I have no need of that hypothesis."

If a behaviorist like Watson were asked where, in his theory of human nature, does the human person come in, he too would, no doubt, reply, with equal lack of humility, "Sir, I have no need of that hypothesis."

❖ ❖

Existentialism boasts of taking people as they are. It ridicules enlightenment for treating people as if they were what they ought to be.

Goethe, the great spokesman of the Enlightenment, seems to have had a premonition of contemporary Existentialism when he said: "If we take people as they are we make them worse. If we treat them as if they were what they ought to be, we help them become what they are capable of being."

❖ ❖

Archibald MacLeish states in a recent book: "It is necessary to believe in man not only as the Christians believe in man, out of duty, or as the democrats believe in man, out of loyalty, but also as the Greeks believed in man, out of pride." That I would amend as follows: "And not only as the Greeks believed in man, out of pride, but also as the ancient Hebrews believed in man, out of faith in God."

❖ ❖

There are two kinds of people: those whose ideas express their personal likes and those whose ideas compensate for their personal lives.

More important than to know what we are is to know what we can do.

It takes the same opportunities and abilities to make us into creative artists of life or reactionary forces hindering its development.

Some people talk a mouthful but say little; others talk little but say a mindful.

The prevalence of the sense of inferiority may be inferred from the way the politicians at election time display their concern for the "common man," "the forgotten man," and "the little man."

To aspire to the heights of reason and spirit is human destiny. Their call is like "the call of the earth's high places."

This is why to be truly human is so much like mountain-climbing.

"A man climbs," writes a famous mountain climber, "because that is the way he is made."

People who can transform hardships into opportunities are like the Eskimos, who keep warm in igloos which they build out of snow and ice.

According to certain anthropologists, the use of metaphors and other circumlocutions originates from the mystic fear which most primitives have of calling things by their real names.

Which shows that it really takes moral courage to call a spade a spade.

In religion as in all other manifestations of human life, there are three distinct stages: experiencing, knowing and understanding.

Most people who have what they call religious experience know as little what they are experiencing as most people know what they experience when they breathe. But even the religious people who know what they are experiencing as religion, understand as little about what they know as most of those who know the workings of an automobile really understand what they know.

Experience involves the body, knowledge the observation and memory, and understanding the interrelation among the things observed and remembered.

If the mind would understand what it knows, and the spirit want what it needs, the body would do what it should.

As mind, spirit and body are interrelated, so are our understanding, our needs and our ideals.

Each of them functions as organicity, polarity and creativity, the three cosmic manifestations of divinity.

There are two kinds of people, those who *stop* to think and those who stop to *think*.

The spiritual advantage of having a bad memory is that we must always be honest and speak the truth. That, by the way, indicates the temptation to which people with good memories are exposed and often yield.

It takes crisis to elicit man's fuller understanding of himself and greater awareness of his higher potentialities.

Women in an audience, listening to a lecture, who knit with their hands sometimes nod with their heads, but seldom knit their brows.

To give way to anger, frustration or hopelessness is to give way to our aggressions and to prevent them from being sublimated into creativity.

14. *Wisdom and Experience*

There are three kinds of thinking: sick thinking, or pessimism; wishful thinking, or optimism; wholesome thinking, or ifism, i.e. if we do what we should what we need will happen.

King Solomon did not become a cynic until he was old. It was then that he wrote *Ecclesiastes*.

Nowadays children begin making cynical wise-cracks before they are out of kindergarten.

The blessings that the wise desire coincide with those that the virtuous deserve.

❖ ❖

The essence of wisdom is to accept one's limitations and to make the most of one's potentialities.

❖ ❖

Not all pessimism is bad. There is a kind which acts like a cathartic.

It should be taken from time to time to purge us of our illusions.

❖ ❖

A proper sense of values is one which enables us so to ration our interests as to frustrate none of them.

❖ ❖

If wisdom were as cheap as courage, there would hardly be any need for courage.

If courage were as rare as wisdom, wisdom would be of no avail.

❖ ❖

Experience is as transferable as imagination.

❖ ❖

Most people learn from experience to repeat the same mistakes.

❖ ❖

There are various ways of escaping the need of attending to some urgent but difficult task.

One of them is to keep on talking about it.

❖ ❖

Without moral courage, all virtue is merely a way of speaking.

❖ ❖

Moral courage is harder than physical courage by as much as the reach of the mind is greater than the reach of the body.

❖ ❖

If the wisdom of outstanding persons had not been overrated, the ordinary person might have exercised the initiative to achieve some wisdom on his own account.

❖ ❖

We don't mind being slaves so long as we are our own slave-drivers.

❖ ❖

Despite what people say when they pray, most of them believe in the god named "Everybody."

All they have to be told is that "Everybody" does it. That settles all questions and puts an end to all arguments.

It takes the courage of a Prometheus to assert one's will against "Everybody."

❖ ❖

If we only knew how to draw the line between an enemy and a disaffected ally, we would know when to be tough and when to be soft.

❖ ❖

No cause can succeed unless it has both brains and guts.

❖ ❖

All too often, in a childish huff, we throw away half the cake, because we cannot have the whole cake.

❖ ❖

The babbit is satisfied with his old illusions.

The radical must have new illusions.

The cynic thinks he can live without illusions.

❖ ❖

Many people are like zeros in that they exercise power not by virtue of what they are, but by virtue of their proximity to a real figure that counts.

❖ ❖

What gives business men their heartaches is that the winds of trade have nothing in them of the steadiness of trade winds, but are more like sudden gusts or hurricanes, defying all calculations.

❖ ❖

There are people who, when they ask you, "What's new?" are really bursting to tell you mainly what's on their own minds.

❖ ❖

Evaluating goods and services in accordance with a money standard facilitates their exchange.

Exchange is one of the most potentially civilized influences.

Yet to make exchange value the measure of all human goods or values is to be blind to their intrinsic worth.

Money is no more a measure of that intrinsic worth than a shadow is a measure of a man's character or career.

❖ ❖

You can never be *for* something without being *against* something.

❖ ❖

If a pessimist is a wet blanket, an optimist is a blanket of artificial grass.

❖ ❖

A sneer is a smear.

❖ ❖

It is an economic fallacy to assume that a peddler is less productive than a puddler. Neither can get along well without the other.

❖ ❖

There are two kinds of people: those who can forgive those whom they have wronged and those who can't.

❖ ❖

Cleverness is a double-edged sword.

Some people are so smart that they are liable to cut themselves.

❖ ❖

If you are typical, you are a subject for science; if you are individual, you are a subject for art; if you are neither, you are average.

❖ ❖

Worse than foolishness is the wrong kind of cleverness.

❖ ❖

Decivilized humans have the viciousness of the uncivilized, implemented by the skill and cunning of the civilized.

❖ ❖

The problems of success are more baffling than those of failure.

❖ ❖

A necessary evil is necessarily the lesser of two evils.

❖ ❖

In a crisis, where survival depends on action free from moral taint, it is better to be a venturesome fool than a timid angel.

❖ ❖

Lord Acton's aphorism that "power corrupts and absolute power corrupts absolutely" is only relatively true.

To say that power corrupts is like saying that desire perverts. Power and desire are only synonyms for life.

The Buddhists drew from that fact the inference that life, as well as desire and power, is evil and that the only good is *nirvana*.

If we refuse to draw such inferences, then we must believe that life, desire, and power are *subject* to corruption—but not that they corrupt.

❖ ❖

Bigotry and piety don't mix.

❖ ❖

A good way of finding out what is meant by religious experience is to try the procedure suggested by the following definition of experience in general:

"Experience is, first of all, doing something; second, doing something that makes a difference; third, knowing what difference it makes."

Try to meet these three requirements with the affirmation of God's unity or with the observance of the Sabbath, and you will know what it means to have religious experience.

❖ ❖

It takes durable values to render life endurable.

❖ ❖

If we want the esthetic enjoyment of both trees and horizons we have to live on a hill.

❖ ❖

By the same token that composers are not ideal interpreters of their own music, autobiographies are less reliable than biographies.

❖ ❖

A purpose is that which helps us live.
It is thus a means as well as an end.

❖ ❖

Frustration is in direct ratio to the square of the distance between promise and fulfillment.

❖ ❖

A day will come to pass when each person will be one person, not many persons.

On that day the Lord will be One and his name One.

❖ ❖

The most tragic waste is unlived life.

❖ ❖

If you have a rendezvous with destiny, be sure to come on time.

❖ ❖

The first prerequisite to the art of living is the ability to budget one's needs and responsibilities in terms of time and money.

❖ ❖

Having failed doesn't mean being a failure.

❖ ❖

It is difficult to recall how even a casual conversation began.

How much more difficult must it be to recall the beginning of a civilization or a religion?

That is why all civilizations and religions begin with legends and myths.

❖ ❖

The difference between optimism and pessimism may be only a difference of emphasis.

Take the sentence, "This is the best of possible worlds." If you are an optimist, you emphasize "best"; if you are a pessimist you emphasize "possible."

❖ ❖

The only paradise men ever lost has been the fool's paradise.

❖ ❖

The evolution of privilege: First it is workable; then it is respectable; then it is immutable; then it is the law of God; then it changes hands and becomes a law of nature.

What makes it workable in the first place is sheer force.

❖ ❖

Only in a world in which objects cast no shadow can blessings be unmixed.

Gratitude is the ability to discount the ingredient of evil in every blessing.

❖ ❖

There are two kinds of resignation:

The wrong kind is to conceive life as fighting a losing war against fate.

The right kind is to conceive life as fighting losing battles but winning the war.

❖ ❖

Last year's floods are of no help against this year's drought.

❖ ❖

Accuracy of vision is of little use without the proper point of view.

❖ ❖

Opportunity combined with danger is the chaos out of which man creates both himself and his world.

❖ ❖

Identifying the element of unreason in human events is the nearest we can get to having them fall into a meaningful pattern.

❖ ❖

The fact that the road to Utopia is always broken up and in need of repairs would not be so bad, if at least there were some detour by which one might finally get there.

❖ ❖

No event is as important as its interpretation.

❖ ❖

Whenever people begin to question the obvious and to boast of their doubting every thing, you may expect an upsurge of obscurantism that is immune to common sense.

❖ ❖

Frequent repetition of an ideal which is not translated into action is a safe investment in laughing-stock.

❖ ❖

The fact that experience seldom entirely vindicates the right does not exempt the right from the need of being tested by experience.

❖ ❖

We shall be able to make as much sense out of life as we put into it.

❖ ❖

The modern version of "vanity of vanities" is "to hell with everything."

Either version is a salve to one's cowardice.

❖ ❖

The advice not to cross a bridge till you get to it is unquestionably sound.

Nevertheless, it is important for anyone who has to map a journey to know ahead of time when and where there is a bridge to be crossed, and what kind of bridge it is.

❖ ❖

A platitude is a truth not geared to anything in particular.

❖ ❖

To do good because its pays is to try the right key on the wrong door.

To do good for its own sake is to try the right door with the wrong key.

To do good because it enhances life's meaning and worthwhileness is to use the right key for the right door.

❖ ❖

The most popular and the most dangerous fallacy is that whatever is indispensable is sufficient.

❖ ❖

There is such a thing as carrying to extremes even the principle of the golden mean.

❖ ❖

Brainless mastery feeds on spineless servitude.

❖ ❖

People should insist on being informed on conditions which have to be reformed.

❖ ❖

Lofty sentiments that are not translated into concrete action have all the fascination of soap bubbles.

❖ ❖

There is a Rabbinic saying that one who is bitten by a snake is frightened at the sight of a rope.

That should remind us that we must not permit our bitter experiences with fanatical religion and insane nationhood to frighten us into assuming that there can be no rational religion nor sane nationhood.

❖ ❖

Without the salt of self-criticism our best efforts are bound to spoil.

❖ ❖

How else than by carrying water on both shoulders can one manage to keep one's balance?

❖ ❖

The tree of good and evil was a tree of knowledge, but not of wisdom.

Knowledge is power, and power may be put to good and evil uses.

But wisdom is the right use of power, and, therefore, can be only good.

❖ ❖

Formerly they used to say, "The rich get richer and the poor get children."

Nowadays the rich get richer and the poor get instruction in how not to have children.

❖ ❖

An intelligent man is one who wants to know *what* in order to know *how*.

A wise man is one who wants to know *what for* in order to know *how*.

❖ ❖

Being wise often requires overcoming the handicap of being learned, for it is difficult for the learned to realize that life is never like what the books describe, nor can it ever be like what the books say it ought to be.

❖ ❖

One does not have to be a bug to be an expert entomologist, nor a drunkard to write a treatise on alcoholism.

❖ ❖

What's wrong with *washing* our dirty linen in public? It only shows we wish to keep clean.

The thing that is wrong is *airing* it.

❖ ❖

If you are in the spotlight, your vision is bound to be circumscribed.

❖ ❖

A progressive idea or reform is like a wedge.

It may be used to lift up or to split apart.

❖ ❖

Any movement, whether political, social or religious, wins adherents more by the fervor of the conduct it inspires than by the doctrines it proclaims.

❖ ❖

Will a horseless age require our saying "If wishes were taxis, beggars would never use the subways?"

❖ ❖

If being bigger meant being better, 'twere better to be elephantine than human.

❖ ❖

The safest refuge from the present has come to be the past.

❖ ❖

Moderation is the art of combining in proper measure attachment to life with detachment from it.

❖ ❖

The mature mind is one that can recognize identity of function and purpose under a variety of ideas and concepts.

❖ ❖

All attempts to revolutionize society as though we were engaged in creating something out of nothing usually end up in repeating long-forgotten mistakes.

❖ ❖

The whole is more than the sum of its parts.
If the parts are bad, the whole is worse than the sum of them.
If the parts are good, it is better than the sum of them.

❖ ❖

By doing we can learn much that we never could learn by merely thinking.

❖ ❖

Because, in our first years, we learn to speak before we think, we have to spend the rest of our lives learning to think before we speak.

❖ ❖

It's not what is learned by heart that counts, but what the heart learns.

❖ ❖

Seeing no bottom to an idea gives the illusion of profundity.

❖ ❖

The mere knowledge of how we might have avoided some tragic mistake is no guarantee that we will not repeat that mistake.

We make out of life what we think it is, because we think of life what we make of it.

The difference between being reactive to experience and being creative with experience is like the difference between the spelling of the words reactive and creative—the same letters but differently arranged—the same activity, but conducted in a different spirit.

The three-dimensional life is one in which due attention is given to each of its three dimensions: its purpose, its means, and its method. Those who live such a life know what to live for, what to live by, and how to live.

To perfect a three-dimensional life will take much longer time than to perfect three-dimensional camera shots.

Potentiality means that neither things nor persons are exhaustively defined by what they are.

The capacity for self-assessment is the beginning of moral wisdom.

When intelligence fails to serve wisdom, it is mastered by folly.

What a man wants first is not necessarily what he wants most.

No truth is ageless for the simple reason that, to be truth, it must speak at least to its own age, and no two ages are alike.

❖ ❖

If we don't sanctify life, we trivialize it.

❖ ❖

There can be no foresight without insight.

❖ ❖

To be wise is to be neither gullible nor cynical.

❖ ❖

All absolutes should be suspect, whether they are based on religious or anti-religious principles.

❖ ❖

A "smart aleck" is one who makes faces at what he cannot face up to.

❖ ❖

The chances of achieving balance in living and thinking are greater, if you know how to take hold of the center of things and ideas.

❖ ❖

People go to the theatre to be entertained, to have a good laugh or a good cry.

Wherein is a good cry entertainment?

A dramatic situation which elicits tears is one which makes us aware that the rest of the world is subject to the same miseries as we are.

In other words, it provides misery with the company it loves.

Or as we Jews say: Our troubles are reduced by half when we realize that everybody has them.

❖ ❖

Gullible people have most reasons to be suspicious—of themselves.

❖ ❖

Don't expect much love from a cynic. Hating himself, how can he love you?

❖ ❖

A rich fool is like a poor painting richly mounted.

❖ ❖

There can hardly be any greater frustration than that which comes from doing those things badly which we want badly to do.

❖ ❖

Intellectual indigestion comes from too much learning and too little intelligence.

❖ ❖

The beginning of wisdom is to take nothing for granted.

❖ ❖

It takes the sensitivity of genius to recognize the significance of the familiar.

❖ ❖

"Man is born free yet he is everywhere in chains," said Rousseau.

That is not true.

What is born is only the promise of man which is first fulfilled when he throws off his chains and becomes free.

❖ ❖

A wishful thinker is one who starts with a conclusion and arrives at an assumption.

❖ ❖

It is true that the whole truth can be arrived at by merely seeing things whole; the parts of things must also not be overlooked.

❖ ❖

No consequence is the consequence of a single event.

❖ ❖

G. B. Shaw often brings down the tragic to the trivial; Kafka generally raises the trivial to the tragic.

❖ ❖

Whether one goes with a bang or a whimper makes a difference only to the survivors.

❖ ❖

The personality we achieve is like the horizon that bounds our view. It depends entirely upon where we stand. It is at its narrowest when we occupy the level of the immediate and the commonplace. It expands as we rise above that level to heights of ever-widening vision.

❖ ❖

The better off we are, the more alive we are.

The more alive we are, the more sensitive we are to suffering and frustration.

The more sensitive we are to suffering and frustration, the more likely we are to wish we were dead.

Hence it follows that the better off we are, the more likely we are to wish we were dead.

This is presumably why Freud saddled us with the "death wish."

Where really is the catch?

The catch is that it is by no means universally true that "the more sensitive we are to suffering and frustration the more likely we are to wish we were dead."

Truly religious people find a zest for living in the very effort to relieve suffering and avert frustration. They feel that, in the long run, God supports them in that effort.

❖ ❖

On the principle that two negatives make an affirmative, the intolerance of intolerance is an affirmative virtue.

❖ ❖

New ideas are born less of difficulties we meet on our way than of those we let ourselves in for.

❖ ❖

Meeting difficulties makes us realize how much better we can do than we thought we could.

❖ ❖

There are two kinds of ideology: seminal and contraceptive. All supernaturalist ideology is definitely contraceptive. It hasn't given birth to a single creative or workable idea.

❖ ❖

The power that creates new responsibilities is never able to catch up with its need for the power to meet them.

❖ ❖

The last thing people learn is to put first things first.

❖ ❖

What doesn't hurt you, you can't know.

❖ ❖

If you wish to act as a bridge between two mutually rival groups, you must expect to be stepped upon by people walking in both directions.

❖ ❖

The spiritual advantage of having a bad memory is that one must always be honest and speak the truth. That, by the way, indicates the temptation to which people with good memories are exposed and, often, yield.

❖ ❖

Thoreau is quoted as having said that when you see a man approach you with the obvious intent of doing you good, you should run for your life.

How do you square that with the mission theory of the Jewish people?

❖ ❖

It takes a bore to stretch an hour into eternity and a wit to crowd eternity into an hour.

❖ ❖

An idea that cannot be translated into terms of the senses does not make sense.

❖ ❖

When men have lost their souls, what will there be left for the times to try?

❖ ❖

Love is not love unless one's entire personality is involved. True love is the enjoyment of responsibility.

❖ ❖

It is not true that the whole truth can be arrived at by merely seeing things whole; the parts of things must also not be overlooked.

❖ ❖

Once the lamb-chop has been burned, putting pink paper frills on it won't make it more edible.

❖ ❖

The policy of muddling through should be avoided not merely because it puts a premium on muddling, but mainly because it cannot guarantee that we shall come through.

❖ ❖

Even natural miracles must not be depended on to happen twice.

They are only good to be remembered, but not to be expected.

If Churchill had understood that in time, he might not have expected the "Miracle of the Marne" to happen a second time, and he might have saved France from surrender.

❖ ❖

Creativity requires the tension between the unifying influence of sentiment and the divisiveness that inheres in freedom of opinion.

❖ ❖

When the exigencies of politics or economics are given a high moral tone, morality's only function gets to be that of window dressing.

❖ ❖

Every long-range program should be translated into immediate objectives. Every immediate objective should be part of a long-range program.

❖ ❖

The future of mankind will be determined not by the use we make of metaphysics but of microphysics, with the immense powers of the nucleus which it places in men's hands.

❖ ❖

If any one complains to you about any idea or philosophy as too abstract for the average person to grasp or too unemotional to become excited about, remind him that money as a medium of exchange is one of the most abstract ideas and yet there are very few things people are more concerned with or excited about than money.

❖ ❖

In life in general, as in the UN, abstaining from a vote is also recorded as a vote.

❖ ❖

Ideas are actually tools, tools of thought.

Some thinkers create one or more particular tools of thought.

The great thinkers have been those who created machine tools which can make any kind of tool.

❖ ❖

Kierkegaard, the apostle of humility, was sure that Jews and liberals could not be humble.

Denouncing people for not being humble is itself a form of arrogance.

❖ ❖

Responsibility is not a ball and chain but an anchor.

❖ ❖

Power without policy is as constructive as a truckload of T.N.T.

Policy without power is as effective as a UN resolution.

❖ ❖

The density of the air which resists the aeroplane in its flight is what makes flight possible.

Thus, the challenges to our ideals are the opportunities for our realizing them.

❖ ❖

Many birds build their nests in nooks of the houses which face the park. Evidently even birds prefer the stability of the artificial environment to the insecurity of the natural environment.

❖ ❖

Joan of Arc was condemned to death, not only because she was an obstinate heretic but also because she dressed like a man and was therefore "possessed of the devil."

It was Frenchmen not Englishmen who condemned her.

Apparently the French had not yet set the style in dress.

❖ ❖

Making a virtue of necessity is not necessarily a vice.

❖ ❖

You cannot defeat defeatism merely with wishful thinking.

❖ ❖

Nothing that is good can remain good unless it is made better.

❖ ❖

Most people's money goes to their head; only in a very few cases does it go to their heart.

❖ ❖

People have always found it easier to flare up for religion, for democracy, for their country, than to define them.

That proves how much easier it is to emote than to think.

❖ ❖

The Talmud records a current popular saying: "Attach yourself to one of high rank and people will bow to you."

❖ ❖

A martyr, whether man or nation, that makes a career of being a martyr is as apt to become a bore, as a veteran who makes a career of being a veteran.

❖ ❖

The method of science is "divide and conquer."
The method of philosophy is "unite and govern."

❖ ❖

Don't try to make history, if you are not prepared to make mistakes in the process.

❖ ❖

The national unemployment rate of several percent may serve as a measuring device, but it is meaningless to individuals who are 100 per cent unemployed.

❖ ❖

What becomes of experience as the criterion of truth when we have two statements like the following, supposedly based on experience: "I have been young and now am old; yet I have never seen the righteous forsaken, or his seed begging bread." The Psalmist

"I who was once young and am old have never seen a stockbroker, or his seed begging bread."
Robert Graves in *The Crowning Privilege*

❖ ❖

Much of what's wrong with the way we live is due to mistaken identity, as when we identify bigness with greatness, price with value, standard of living with standard of life.

❖ ❖

If knowledge alone were sufficient, physicians, especially geriatricians, ought to be the most long-lived people.

❖ ❖

If I have to choose between stuffiness and a vacuum, I choose stuffiness.

❖ ❖

You have to go through the baptism of fire if you want to be spared the baptism of being fired.

❖ ❖

You have to square ideals with realities.

❖ ❖

Some, after liberating themselves from one hostile environment, create or find new hostile environments and so are never spiritually or emotionally liberated.

❖ ❖

Going on with life as usual is not an absolute value; it can sometimes be most destructive.

❖ ❖

Youth rides in the cab of the locomotive and jubilantly surveys the track ahead. Age rides in the observation car and gazes back with sweet sorrow upon the fading scenes of the past.

Don't sit in the observation car with folded hands, gazing back upon the fading scenes of the past. Force yourself to turn your eyes and seek new experiences.

❖ ❖

It requires a titanic scorning of delights to live laborious days.

❖ ❖

Every thought one has acquires a voice independent of one and conducts an internal dialogue.

❖ ❖

The saddest aspect of old age is to have outlived one's contemporaries.

❖ ❖

What we don't know is more likely to harm us than what we do know.

❖ ❖

The following ad adorns some New York buses:

Headache? Take aspirin.

Tension? Take Compoz.

Jewish tradition prescribed different care.

Headache? Study Torah.

Tension? Engage in good deeds.

❖ ❖

A wife who is a help-meet always cooks and bakes for her husband and herself. A wife who is a help-eat always cooks and bakes mainly for her husband.

❖ ❖

If the purpose of education is to inculcate a sense of reality, it must make provision for enough courage not to run away from reality when it is actually sensed.

Meeting difficulties makes us realize how much better we can do than we thought we could.

When it comes to being treated with love and respect it is well to remember that grown-ups are entitled to it as much as children.

Only when we improve life can we find life worthwhile. That is because we love whatever we improve.

One of the most dangerous purposes of human life is improvement to end all need for further improvement.

Boswell tells us of the clergyman who said that he too had tried to be a philosopher, but that cheerfulness would keep breaking in.

The case with Kohelet, as he himself tells us, was the reverse. He tried with all his might to be cheerful, but philosophy kept breaking in.

To be a confirmed pessimist one has to enjoy one's own *weltschmerz*.

To be wanted is to be happy; to be needed is to be on the way to fulfillment.

If life is meant to be lived as an art, then most people's lives are more like doodling than like art.

II. RELIGION

1. *God*

The more people were concerned with supernaturalist religion, the less was supernaturalist religion concerned with people.

❖ ❖

Religion is conscience weighted with a sense of history.

❖ ❖

Most theological disputes are as little evocative of truth as the threshing of straw is evocative of grain.

❖ ❖

We do not need to establish metaphysically the freedom of the human will when we urge people to take care of their physical health.

Why should it be necessary when we urge them to take care of their mental and spiritual health?

❖ ❖

A concrete case of what is meant by religion as an opiate is the village where Ignazio Silone was born and which he describes as follows:

"The condition of human existence has always been particularly difficult there; pain has always been accepted there as first among the laws of nature, and the Cross honored and welcomed because of it."

❖ ❖

Bad religion is a half truth.

That is why it is worse than no religion, which is a whole lie.

Communism is dangerous, not because it is atheistic, but because it is *bad religion*.

A good example of bad religion is also the case of the Cardinals during the scandalous fifteenth century. When they came to celebrate the coronation of the Pope, they brought along their own butlers and their own wines to make sure they wouldn't be poisoned.

❖ ❖

It's all up with a sacred cow when it begins to act like a *scared* cow.

❖ ❖

The department stores have far more effective ways of popularizing religious festivals than the churches or synagogues.

❖ ❖

A religion that asks much gets something; a religion that asks little gets nothing.

❖ ❖

Whatever we yearn for most is our religion—whether it be salvation, power or fame.

The organization or institution which helps us to get what we yearn for most is our church or synagogue—whether it be the house of God, the exchange, the market place, the academy, the labor organization, the fraternal order, the luncheon club.

❖ ❖

To refuse to have anything to do with religion because of the abuses to which it is subject is like refusing to breathe because the air is full of harmful germs.

❖ ❖

"War is too important," said Clemenceau, "to be left to the generals."

By the same token, religion is too important to be left to the theologians.

❖ ❖

Opiates are modern man's religion, and escapism his morality.

❖ ❖

Religion will denote culture when culture is dealt with as religion.

❖ ❖

Piety is no more free from the competitive spirit than business.

❖ ❖

We do religion a disservice when we advertise it as a kind of aspirin with which to cure all of mankind's headaches.

❖ ❖

The most dangerous counterfeiters are not those who make bogus money but those who falsify the sense of the great words that pass for ethical and religious currency.

❖ ❖

The so-called religious renaissance of our times is little more than a nostalgic literary cult which is an escape from the complexities of civilization, like the literary cult of the simple life during the 18th century.

❖ ❖

When a water system is run for the benefit of politicians, it does not occur to us to deny the indispensability of water.

Yet, when a religious organization is either corrupt or mismanaged, we conclude that we can get along without religion.

❖ ❖

Religion is like the windshield of an automobile.

When we pass through a rainstorm of trying experience, it is important to keep the windshield wiper of common sense working. Otherwise religion will only shut out the view ahead.

If a religionless life is like skimmed milk, the best kind of religious life is like homogenized milk.

In such a life the religious element cannot be skimmed off the secular.

❖ ❖

Religious terms like *God, salvation, sin, merit, heaven, hell,* are like algebraic symbols.

To make sense they must each have a definite meaning and be mutually consistent on the basis of that meaning.

❖ ❖

One has to be childish to play God. Only the childlike can be Godlike.

❖ ❖

Scientific progress is no more responsible for the decline in religion than progress in medicine for the many new ailments with which we have become familiar.

❖ ❖

A religion that teaches masochistic doctrine is all too likely to lead to sadistic practices.

❖ ❖

The synagogue or church conception of religion is a first cousin to the museum conception of art.

❖ ❖

What patrioteering is to patriotism, religiosity is to religion.

❖ ❖

Theology is to religion what esthetic criticism is to art.

❖ ❖

Those who wish to feel that they are justified in not bothering with religion are the first to resent all attempts to defrost the traditional notions of religion.

❖ ❖

As a rule, the only bone theologians throw to common sense is a bone of contention.

There is a psychological connection between torturing the words of Scripture into proclaiming the doctrine of the Church, and torturing heretics into submission to the authority of the Church.

In a religious age or environment, priests sanction the *status quo*. In an irreligious age, philosophers and scientists rationalize it.

Sovietism was once a Stalin-intoxicated religion.

G. B. Shaw said: "There is only one religion, though there are a thousand versions of it."

That makes as much and as little sense as saying: "There is only one language, though there are two thousand versions of it."

Kafka anticipated the incredible lengths to which human beings could carry their sadistic tendencies. He articulated that anticipation in his book, *The Trial*.

He seems also to have foreseen the ludicrous lengths to which people would carry their cultic tendencies and make a religion of him. That is probably why he asked to have his writings burned.

Plutarch was the first to use the term "theologian."

In describing the oracle at Delphi he tells of the priestess, who, after having fallen into a trance, would utter some meaningless sounds, which were then translated into meaningful verse by "theologians."

Ever since then it has come to be applied to one who interprets a religious tradition which has ceased to have meaning for most people.

What we ordinarily speak of as the fragmentizing effect of civilization upon human life is, in the language of religion, referred to as the Fall of Man.

As with Humpty Dumpty, who had a great fall, all the king's horses and all the king's men cannot put civilized man together again.

But what the king's horses and the king's men cannot do, the King himself can do.

That is why we need religion.

In human experience, God appears under various disguises, some of which seem as though they were intended to keep us guessing whether He exists at all.

Organized religion is supposed to be the one disguise which is to do nothing more than to prevent us from being blinded by His glory.

Actually, however, organized religion often has the effect of blinding us to His glory.

A good deal of religious controversy consists in quarreling over bottles that have long been emptied of their wine.

❖ ❖

We generally assume that religion is or should be eventually a personal affair.

According to the late philosopher, Alfred N. Whitehead, religion is "what the individual does with his solitariness."

We are aware, of course, of the existence of public religion, but we discount its value.

We think of public religion as formal and mechanical and as an expression of the human tendency to act in herds.

The truth is that public religion is as much of a prerequisite to personal religion as conversation is to individual thought.

We would hardly suggest doing away with conversation because it is marked by confusion of ideas and inadequate expression.

Public religion—or religion expressed and lived by whole societies of human beings, however abounding in superstition, error, and mechanical conformity—is the matrix of the most exalted and inspired achievements in individual religion.

Most people want their religion pure and undefined.

To try to separate a religion from the civilization to which it belongs is like trying to separate weight from body.

Men of God tend to mistake their fear of one another for the fear of God, and their love of God for the love of their fellowman.

The trouble with theologians is that they assume that God waits for the theologians to make up His mind for Him.

That a bigot considers himself "religious" should make us wary of using that term in an honorific sense.

If religion were more generally recognized as a realm of inarticulate groping, instead of being regarded as a realm of articulate griping, we might have made more headway in it.

"Atheism, that is to say, deepest doubt," according to Paul Tillich, "induces in religion a radical tension and thus preserves it from stagnation."

According to the late Rabbi Isaac Kook of Jerusalem, "Atheism does to conventional religion what an electric storm does to the air. It purifies and freshens it."

What really is the difference between the priest and the prophet, and what do they hold in common?

The priest believes in standing still; the prophet believes in being in a hurry.

Both agree that the pedestrian is a nuisance because he insists on walking and taking his time.

Whatever else religious beliefs are, they are certainly events in a people's history.

When a historian like Toynbee begins to theologize, we get a theology as crude as would be the history written by a theologian like Barth.

There should be a trade law demanding an itemization of all ingredients that go into the making of the average man's religion. Such an itemization would probably read as follows:

Grandmother's notions about God, the religious school's stories of things that never happened, the memories both bothersome and pleasant of ceremonials, like confirmation and marriage, or gloomy, like those of funerals, and the interminable series of sermons which sought to divert the mind from the immediate concerns of life.

Religion should be a series of self-corrective attempts on the part of man to become fully human.

We short-circuit religion when we treat it purely as an affair between the individual and God. To function normally, the religious current connecting the individual with God must pass through the life of a people.

A provincial dialect, when used by a great poet, becomes a national language. This was the case with the Tuscan dialect, which became nationalized through Dante's writings. Likewise a national religion becomes universalized when a great prophet makes it the medium of his teaching.

Spiritual goods pine away from non-consumption.

So long as religion is the trade of the clergy, trade will be the religion of the laity.

If money is, as Keynes puts it, what the state says it is, then morals are what the church says they are.

It is, therefore, no wonder that with the separation of church and state, money is money and morals are morals, and the twain seldom meet.

There is a vacuum in Jewish theological thinking in our day, and Christian thinking is rushing in to fill it. Otto, Barth, Niebuhr and Maritain have a strange fascination for some Jewish theologians.

Instead of the Jewish doctrine of man's ability to transform himself and the world by dint of his freedom of the will, some Jewish thinkers are captivated by Protestant thinking: "Whom

God would save He first makes fit." This sounds like the obverse of the pagan doctrine: "Whom the gods would destroy, they first make mad."

Would it not be wiser to evolve a Jewish theology which places on man the full responsibility for the kind of world we are to live in?

❖ ❖

To know how to go about making a religion into what it ought to be we must have a real understanding of what goes into the making of a religion.

The distinction between the holy and the profane is not like the distinction between the religious and the secular, for the simple reason that the religious is not always holy nor the secular always profane.

The distinction between the holy and the religious is like the distinction between value and price, or between greatness and bigness.

❖ ❖

To expect the Synagogue to make mean people kind or selfish people generous is like expecting an art museum to open the eyes of the blind.

The Psalmist did *not* say:
"Who shall have clean hand and a pure heart?
He that shall ascend the Mount of the Lord
And he that shall stand in His holy place."

❖ ❖

Benzine is good for cleaning purposes. But the trouble with it is that it is inflammable and explosive. Treated chemically, however, it can be rendered harmless, and yet retain its usefulness.

Religion too is an excellent soul-cleanser, but inflammable and mightily explosive at the least provocation. Let us so treat it intellectually as to deprive it of its dangerous qualities, while taking care to preserve its cleansing properties.

❖ ❖

The negation of philosophy is also a philosophy.
The negation of religion is also a religion.

❖ ❖

A "pious resolution" is a resolution we don't do anything about.
So that's what people think of piety?

❖ ❖

Miracle religion has nothing to do with ordinary human feelings. A medieval saint, Angela of Foligno, whose sainthood was based on the alleged performance of miracles, congratulated herself on the death of her mother, husband and children, whom she described "as great obstacles in the way of God."

❖ ❖

The best cure for a sense of guilt is a sense of duty.

❖ ❖

Chrysostom, one of the Greek Fathers of the Church, maintained that any one who preached as his own sermons written by someone else was not guilty of plagiarism, if he lived up to the teachings of those sermons.
Apparently Chrysostom did not expect sermons to have anything to say about stealing.

❖ ❖

The religious instinct, left to itself, is no more reliable than the mother instinct.
In China and India the mother instinct kills off one baby out of every two.

With the aid of organized intelligence, however, the mother instinct in America saves ninety-five or more out of every hundred children.

Likewise, with the aid of organized intelligence, the religious instinct would save the greater portion of mankind for the kind of human life which that instinct is providentially intended to evolve.

Some people, when they find it hard to believe in miracles as the essence of religion, find it necessary to put in their place ritual practices that entail sacrifice.

Their notion of religion is that it cannot be real unless it puts on the screws somewhere—if not on the mind, then on the body.

A religious institution that is interested in maintaining the religious status quo, which is one of outer conformity and inner lack of conviction, should recruit students with a diplomatic type of mind.

If, however, it is interested in revitalizing religion, it should seek out students who have the most original and inquiring minds.

Much of the present upsurge in religious affiliation, which is mistaken for religious revival, is due to the eagerness not to be suspected of having been contaminated by Communism.

The separation of society and religion is about as successful a compromise as would be the separation of stomach and heart.

❖ ❖

Only an other-worldly religion can manage to remain unchanging in a changing world.

Only a religion based on supernaturalism can dodge the moral imperatives of nature's God.

Religious revivalists act very much like hospital nurses who wake their patients to give them sleeping pills.

Matthew Arnold defined religion as morality touched with emotion.

Historically, religion has been emotion touched with morality, and sometimes not even touched.

Most people's religion is no more functional than ornamental scrollwork in architecture.

We must educate ourselves in the process of defrosting the great concepts in the religious tradition of mankind.

That process would carry us very far toward a better understanding of the great books of the past, to say nothing of a better ability to understand one another.

Americans who "trust in God" and distrust "brain trusts" apparently believe in the separation of religion from brains.

Most people assume that religion is a retreat from reality. That is why, when reality gets to be too uncomfortable to live with, they take to religion.

As soon as a religion becomes disengaged from its civilization, both become subject to corruption.

When the electric lights don't work, we use candles.
When the refrigerator is out of commission, we send for ice.
When our lives get out of order, we try religion.

❖ ❖

Not all religion is good, and not all nationalism is bad.

❖ ❖

Most theologians regard religion as a solution threatened by a problem.

❖ ❖

Theologians who wrestle with the problem of evil might as well wrestle with the problem of why a stick has two ends instead of one.

❖ ❖

We can learn from theology more about the nature of man than about the nature of God.

❖ ❖

Existentialism is either/or, as Kierkegaard entitled his first work. It is either supernaturalism, which Kierkegaard himself stressed, or it is atheism which Sartre stresses. It is either totalitarianism or anarchy. Religion is either absolute or obsolete.

Someone ought to write a book entitled "Neither."

❖ ❖

There is something of the huckster spirit in the glee with which some members of the clergy hail the so-called religious upsurge.

❖ ❖

The trouble with controversies in religion and politics is not the heat but the humidity; so much of it is "all wet."

❖ ❖

The millenium will come when mankind learns to be half as afraid of the scientific hell of its own invention as it was for centuries of the theological hell of its own imagination.

❖ ❖

An intelligent and instructed laity is as indispensable for the teaching of sound religion as for the practice of sound medicine.

For lack of such laity various kinds of religious quackery are peddled around and bought up at bargain prices.

A secularist is one for whom "first and last things" are the first things he forgets and the last things he thinks about.

The difference between philosophy and religion is like the difference between the dentist's knowledge of a toothache and the patient's knowledge of it. The former is essential knowledge; the latter existential knowledge.

Therefore, philosophy without religion is like a dentist without a patient, and religion without philosophy is like a patient who has no dentist to cure his pain.

Genuine religion is so integral a part of politics, economics and culture that to try to extract it from them and to institutionalize it is like trying to extract a hole from a doughnut and make it into a subject for geometry.

Ever since religion has been in trouble it has been in search of a definition.

Both religion and reason began their careers by being accessories after the fact.

Human progress consists in transforming them into agents responsible for the fact.

A people without learning is a people without a mind.

A people without the arts is a people without a heart.
A people without religion is a people without a soul.

❖ ❖

The immaturity of any culture betrays itself with what it does with its folk religion. By that test American culture has not yet come of age.

For example, the Thanksgiving Day parade in New York empties all churches and synagogues of worshipers.

The business exploitation of infantile interests and tastes, which enables such a parade to steal a march on the historic religions, sooner or later marches men off to the wars.

❖ ❖

Some theologians succeed in making actual theophobes out of potential theophiles.

❖ ❖

The antithesis of religious universalism is not particularism but exclusivism.

❖ ❖

The function of religion is to enable us to get a view of life that is larger than life.

❖ ❖

Other-worldly religion conceived its task as that of salvaging individual lives which are wrecked on the shore of this world.

This-worldly religion conceives its task as that of building a breakwater and providing a harbor for storm-tossed ships, so that human lives shall not have to be wrecked.

❖ ❖

The main function of institutional religion should not be to win new adherents but to improve its old adherents.

❖ ❖

A generation or two ago most people took it for granted that science was inherently in conflict with religion.

Nowadays the same kind of conflict is assumed to exist between secularism and religion.

The truth is that it depends entirely on the kind of science or secularism one has in mind.

Only the science which oversteps its bounds and the secularism which usurps the place of religion are hostile to religion.

No idea or belief means anything unless it makes an identifiable difference in your other ideas or beliefs. That is the only genuine definition of pragmatism.

The moment you make a statement about God, man or the world, pragmatism calls you to the witness stand of your own mind and begins to cross-examine you, to make sure that you know what you are talking about. If, in answering the questions which pragmatism puts to you, you contradict yourself, your statement is justly discredited.

That explains why pragmatism is unpopular. Yet, what would we do in the courts without good trial lawyers?

Organized religion has been quite content to rest with God the case of human equality and dignity, instead of taking the trouble to give them mundane reality.

That is borne out in a little book called *Church Union* by John R. Scotford, where we read the following:

"The churches of the average community fall into three groups. First are the society churches: Episcopal, Presbyterian, Congregational, Unitarian (in New England). Then there are the churches of the common people: Methodist, Baptist, Disciples, Lutheran. Last come the other-side-of-the-tracks churches: Church of God, Nazarene, Pentecostal, foreign-language speaking."

When organized religion succeeds in organizing snobbishness, we shall have the Kingdom of God.

Religion is not intended to answer the ultimate questions of existence. It can only provide an effective protection against their shattering impact.

Those who deplore any attempt to raise religion to a high intellectual level on the ground that it is bound to alienate the common man from religion, at heart despise the common man—they regard him as too stupid to think. They have a cynical idea of religion—they regard its main function as being that of keeping the common man under control.

The current religious revival is nothing but a mirage of order in a desert of moral chaos.

The kind of existentialism that religion needs is the kind that would urge us to *remove* the evils that afflict mankind instead of trying to *interpret* them.

On shipboard only second-class passengers seem to be interested in religious accommodations. First-class passengers have too many other accommodations to miss those. Third-class passengers are so lacking in any that they have no mind for those.

Religion is not a cloak but a spirit.

We Jews can least afford to identify religion with clericalism.

As long as our people was a theocracy, the synagogue was coextensive with our peoplehood.

Now that our people can survive only as a democracy, it is inevitable for additional sources of authority and cultural influence to arise as agencies of our peoplehood.

Let the synagogue cultivate its own garden, and beware of wasting its energies and jeopardizing Jewish life by starting a *Kulturkampf* in our midst.

Man's physical self abides in space; his spiritual self in time.

Technology enables man to span space; religion, to span the ages.

Formerly the main sustaining force of religion was ignorance. Nowadays it has to be knowledge.

That explains why there was little irreligion in the past, and why there is so much nowadays.

From being an opiate for the masses, religion has come to be an opiate for the classes.

It affords them the bliss which comes from ignoring the social explosives they are laying up for themselves.

The so-called religious revival is religion illuminated by the phosphorescence of its own decay.

If the idea of brotherhood managed to survive as a source of inspiration despite all the bloody-brother stories in life and literature, why may not religion survive as the hope of mankind, despite all the crimes committed in the name of religion?

An evangelist is a preacher who pulpitates, with a view to get the hearts of his audience to palpitate.

Most people come out of religious services with a sense of relief similar to that which they feel when the recorded music has stopped and the airplane is ready for the take-off.

❖ ❖

Divinity is not *in* us but *through* us.

❖ ❖

What is needed in order to grasp the total and divine character of existence is not a leap of faith, which is only liable to land one in the abyss of despair, but the ability to throw the grand loop that can bring together essence and existence, matter and spirit, nature and God.

❖ ❖

May it not be that divinity is like the opaque side of the mirror of morality in which man sees his own image?

He has scarcely outgrown the childish tendency to look for the man behind the mirror.

It will take him a long time to realize that without divinity he would not know himself as man, but that does not mean that God resembles man or is merely the projection of man's father image.

❖ ❖

There were buses in New York which carried signs reading, "This bus does not go to the New Puerto Rico Hotel in the Riviera."

Such signs remind one of the kind of negative theology which keeps on stressing what God is not. He is not cruel, vindictive, etc. It does that because it has nothing to say about what God is or how to get to Him.

❖ ❖

Of man's soul, spirit or conscience, we are told that it is the lamp of the Eternal (Prov. 20:27). The author of that statement undoubtedly conceived the Eternal as a personal being.

That statement is even more appropriate concerning the soul, spirit or conscience, with the Eternal as the Process that makes for man's salvation or fulfillment. Think of the electric bulb which is the lamp of the electric current.

God as the Power that makes for human fulfillment manifests Himself through growth in body, mind and character of a child at play.

Why, then, do so few grown persons permit God to manifest Himself in like manner in their practical affairs and dealings with one another?

God will have established His Kingdom when religion and nationalism are made safe for the world.

The Rabbis say that, in the process of creating the world, God had to destroy many worlds which failed to meet His approval.

Which means that all creativity implies experimentation and resort to trial and error.

An ambassador is only such so long as he represents the government of his country.

Man is man only so long as he properly represents the Divine Government of the world.

The structure of a sea-shell is a far more reliable proof of the existence of the sea than the murmur of the sea which you are supposed to hear when you put a sea-shell to your ear.

By the same token, one can find greater proof of God's existence in the aspiration of man than in the reports of His self-revelation.

Man's discovery of God is God's self-revelation to man.

❖ ❖

The reason we find it difficult to think of God except in human-like terms like "personal" or "loving" is that, if we think of God at all, it is because we are haunted by the will to become fully human.

❖ ❖

Religion should illuminate experience, not reflect it.

❖ ❖

When a person deifies himself—we get tyranny.
When a nation deifies itself—we get chauvinism.
When a class deifies itself—we get totalitarianism.
When a church deifies itself—we get clericalism.
All these are forms of idolatry.

Idolatry, as the deification of some particular embodiment of power, whether natural or human, is incomparably more prevalent than atheism.

What we seldom recognize is that the evil consequences of idolatry are greater than those of atheism.

Yet the Jewish tradition seems to have sensed that fact: The Ten Commandments prohibit idolatry, but make no mention of atheism. Further, among the seven laws which are recognized as universal (i.e., commanded to all the descendants of Noah), the law against idolatry is included, but there is no law among them against atheism.

❖ ❖

To affirm with the religious philosophers that God is an incorporeal being is to affirm a paradox.

An incorporeal being is as contradictory as a square circle.

To be real, and at the same time incorporeal, God has to be conceived as process.

Fire is nevertheless real for being a process and not a thing, a process of oxidation and not a substance like water. Although the ancients thought it was a thing, they realized that it had certain qualities that set it apart from mere things.

That is why the Pharisees regarded fire as divine, and the Stoics spoke of God as the primary fire immanent in the world.

Fire is one of the many processes of becoming, but God is the all-inclusive process of creating.

The best argument for the existence of God is a godlike human life.

It is just as wrong not to use God's name when it can help to give a lift to the human spirit as to use God's name in vain.

We do not owe our sense of responsibility to our belief in God as much as we owe our belief in God to our sense of responsibility.

There is as much hollow pretense in religion for religion's sake, or in virtue for virtue's sake, as there is in art for art's sake.

Nothing is whole or good unless it is *for life's sake.*

That is what our sages meant when they urged that all our works should be for God's sake.

In the last instance, it is nature that heals, not medicine; God saves, not religion.

❖ ❖

Scientific assumptions of the origin of religion are generally in the same class with the assumption that the waving of the trees makes the wind.

Thus the assumption that fear is the source of the belief in gods overlooks the fact that fear itself is an expression of the will to live and therefore a manifestation of God as the power that makes for life.

❖ ❖

John Foster Dulles once had occasion to repeat the following stereotype:

"Belief in the dignity and worth of the individual flows from the assumption that the individual is created by God in His image."

That is like saying that we dress well in order to look at a mirror.

The dignity and worth of the individual is a moral axiom or ultimate which religion expresses by saying, "God created Man in His image."

❖ ❖

When the philosophers call God "The Absolute" they misname Him.

The Absolute is without a sense of humor.

Of God, however, it is said, "He that sitteth in heaven laugheth."

❖ ❖

A concept of God is like a horizon at which the furthest reaches of our vision meet the infinite spaces beyond.

A concept of society corresponds to all of human life within the scope of our own vision.

A concept of self is like the eye, which, seeing all else, does not see itself.

❖ ❖

To want to know where the self ends and God begins is like wanting to know where the musician ends and the music begins.

❖ ❖

A beautiful soul is an image of God, as a fine canvas is an image of a landscape.

The most skillful copy of the finest canvas cannot compare with a painting directly from nature.

This is why the Torah would have us "imitate" God directly, and not any of His incarnations.

If we succeeded in canceling out the tumult of the outside world and wrapped ourselves in the silence of our own solitariness, we would hear faintly something like a far-away hum.

What might that sound be?

Some say it is caused by the molecules hitting the eardrums.

Others would think it was due to the coursing of the blood stream.

To a Jew it would be something like "the sound of the thin stillness" during which Elijah heard the voice of God.

To behold God in man, we have to learn to see the universal in the individual and the eternal in the temporal.

High school students are taught nowadays to get the meaning of words from their use in sentences.

Thus, a far better way of learning the meaning of God than consulting works on the philosophy and psychology of religion would be to note how the word God is used in prayers and sacred writings.

Though God is perfect, He is not a perfectionist.

Otherwise, how would Abraham have dared to plead with God not to destroy the wicked cities of Sodom and Gomorrah, even if only ten righteous men were to be found there?

According to our sages, Abraham is supposed to have addressed God thus: "Unless Thou foregoest a little, the world cannot survive."

❖ ❖

People will begin to return to God when they realize that they can be far nearer to Him when alive than when they are dead.

❖ ❖

There is much that religious thought can learn from political thought.

In pre-modern times no one could imagine sovereignty except as embodied in a visible king or prince.

At long last we are getting used to the notion of sovereignty as the general will that resides in a people.

The same is true with regard to the idea of God. The average person found it hard to dissociate godhood from a mental image of a magnified man.

❖ ❖

By now we are beginning to realize that godhood is the process within and without mankind that makes for its salvation.

By the same token that we dread insanity and repel moral disintegration within ourselves, we dread the thought of a world governed by mere chance, and repel the assumption of a meaningless and Godless universe.

❖ ❖

Many people who find the traditional conception of God as "worker of miracles" untenable, become atheists. They cannot understand a concept of God in which He is regarded as working in and through nature. They say you have no right to change the meaning of the term "God."

One wonders what they would say about the term "atom." It used to be considered the smallest possible particle of matter.

The very term means, from the Greek, an uncuttable portion of matter. Now that we can split the atom, shall we give up the term?

Why not extend the same privilege of redefinition to the term "God"? Henceforth it should mean the Power that makes for the realization of human destiny.

The legend of Abraham's breaking the idols in his father's house implies that rejecting the image we have of God is often a necessary prerequisite to our serving the true God.

Someone was quoted as saying: "The question is no longer whether we can believe in God, but whether and in what sense we can believe in man."

Actually they are one and the same question, because man and God are correlative terms, as may be gathered from the statement in the Torah that man was made in the image of God.

God is the goad that impels man to become fully human.

Nietzsche points out that "a thought comes when it wishes, not when I wish."

That is why a prophet who experiences the compulsory character of his message is right in ascribing his message to God.

Man proposes, the theologian imposes, and God disposes.

The God-impulse in us is not fear but hope, not helplessness but self-help, not despondency but courage, not the obfuscation of the mind but the light of reason, not the belittlement of what man is but the exaltation of what he might be.

People belong to a religion not because they believe in God but because they want to believe in God.

That want cannot be met by repeating what God meant to the ancients.

What made sense to them does not necessarily make sense to us.

❖ ❖

In Jewish tradition, "The Place" is sometimes used as a synonym for "God."

Philo, the ancient Jewish philosopher of Alexandria, says the reason God is called "The Place" is that "He Himself occupies Himself or is full of Himself."

That explains why some people we know think they are God.

❖ ❖

Theologians usually make it their business to tell us that we don't have to know what or who God is in order to believe in Him.

But they have no right to tell us that we are likewise excused from knowing what it means to believe in God.

❖ ❖

The command to love one's neighbor is to love the Divinity which is in him.

❖ ❖

As the salt of the body fluids reminds us of the sea that is within us and around us, so should the love that is in our hearts remind us of the Divinity that is within us and around us.

❖ ❖

Our God idea is as much like the God idea of our ancient forefathers as the jet plane is like the waxen wings of Icarus that melted in the sun. The myth of Icarus attempting flight in the air as the work of the imagination was the necessary forerunner of the jet plane which is the work of creative intelligence.

Thus, without idolatry and mythology as the first expressions of religion we should not have arrived at a rational idea of God.

❖ ❖

The idea of God is a map of the Cosmos. It selects those features of the Cosmos that enable man to become fully human.

It is no more subjective than a map which locates only the mountains, rivers and cities.

❖ ❖

The difference between the ancient man's conception of God and the modern man's stands out clearly in the change that has taken place in men's ideas about mountain climbing.

High mountains were never scaled until about a century or two ago, because of the vague fear that the deities or spirits dwelling on their summits might resent man's intrusion.

Nowadays, when a *Times* correspondent reports the achievements on Everest, he adds: "True mountaineers the world over know that no one conquered Everest, but a company of brave hearts, under God."

Evidently, a great change has come over men's ideas of God.

❖ ❖

The realities that count most in human life are generally intangible, invisible, imponderable; but they cannot be realities if they are ineffable. If we can say nothing about something except that we can say nothing about it, it can play no role whatever in our conscious life. It simply doesn't exist for us. That is why we must avoid speaking of God as ineffable.

❖ ❖

When we speak of God's attributes, we should mean not that God *has* those attributes but that He *is* those attributes.

The difference between God's *having* and God's *being* His attributes is the difference between the popular but mistaken conception of God as a distinct entity and the difficult but tenable conception of God as process.

❖ ❖

Mankind has been brought up in want-centered religion. Its gods have been conceived as want-fulfilling powers.

The transition to need-centered religion is bound to be slow and painful, the need in question being that of becoming a human person.

God's Kingdom will be established on earth when God comes to be known as the Power that is need-impelling and need-fulfilling.

❖ ❖

Man may be the measure of all things, but God is the measure of measure.

❖ ❖

The Psalmist recommends (Ps. 34): "Try God." Perhaps we ought to experiment with the belief in God.

For all we know, it might yield us amazing results.

We might experiment, for example, with the assumption that God is the Power that can help us to be honest.

Every time we are about to speak or write what we know to be untrue, let us repeat to ourselves the prayer, "O God, make me a clean heart."

❖ ❖

The description of tragic accidents, the high rate of infant mortality, and raging epidemics as "acts of God" is an alibi for human negligence and ignorance.

❖ ❖

"Be as servants who serve their masters not for the sake of reward" (*Pirke Abot* 1:3).

The truth of this becomes evident in the light of recent psychological analysis of human conduct. A distinction is drawn between pragmatic and expressive behavior. Pragmatic behavior is purposive. It looks to gratification, whether physical or mental, whether in the form of satisfying the hunger for food and safety or the need for love and respect. Expressive behavior comes spontaneously and is unmotivated by the prospect of reward.

The true artist works in the spirit of expressive behavior, whether it be in the fine arts or in the art of living.

The true artist in the art of living worships God because he cannot do otherwise. It is an end in itself, for through it he expresses his true self.

❖ ❖

The Sage in *Proverbs* says:

"A man's own follies pervert his course; then he rages against God."

The poet in the *Odyssey* has Zeus say: "How vainly mortal men do blame the gods. Of us, they say, comes evil, but through the blindness of their hearts they bring sorrow on themselves."

❖ ❖

The bafflement and frustration which are part of every person's life are evidence of the inexhaustible possibilities for good that inhere in the human being.

These possibilities indicate that it is man's destiny to transcend himself.

The drive to self-transcendence is perhaps the best means of experiencing the reality of God.

❖ ❖

By and large we don't do what we ought to, or what is best for us, unless we have to.

How, then, does what we ought to do or what is best for us ever get done?

Evidently we are not as bad as we think we are.

❖ ❖

Learn to arrive at your loyalty to mankind via your family and your nation rather than past them, and at your loyalty to God via mankind rather than past it.

2. *Naturalism & Supernaturalism*

The neo-supernaturalists—both Jewish and Christian—make it a point to refer to eighteenth century rationalism as the source of outlived banalities.

Yet it is to those banalities that we owe the idea of inalienable rights to life, liberty and the pursuit of happiness, the dignity of the individual not only before God but also before his fellow men, and other ameliorations of the human condition.

No wonder most of us prefer one of those rationalist banalities to a dozen of the supernaturalist absurdities.

❖ ❖

The Jewish universe of discourse has been swamped by the tidal wave of modernism and has broken up into noncommunicating islands.

❖ ❖

Supernaturalism is the backwater whence arise the illusions that befog us.

❖ ❖

Otherworldliness is defeatism and asceticism is escapism.

❖ ❖

RELIGION   157

The naturalist reinterpretation of religion is best exemplified by the well known story concerning Mohamet. He had boasted that with faith and prayer he could make a mountain come to him. When he put his boast to a test and failed he calmly said: "Well, if the mountain will not come to Mohamet, Mohamet will go to the mountain."

If the important thing is for the mountain and Mohamet to get together, what difference does it really make which goes to whom?

Supernaturalism is bound to seem authentic or valid so long as the mind lacks experience of naturalism as a basis for comparison.

Supernaturalism is animism in its final phase.

3. Salvation

Whatever is *Ad Majorem Humani Salutem* (for the greater glory of man) is *Ad Majorem Dei Gloriam* (for the greater glory of God).

Since man can transform himself and his fellows into creatures that are *inferior* to the beasts of the field, why may he not by the same token transform himself and his fellows into human beings that are *superior* to the beasts of the field?

❖ ❖

When theologians gloat over the failure of "salvation by science," they forget two things. First, science never promised to bring salvation: it only promised to create the *conditions* necessary to salvation, and it has kept its promise. Second, theology, ever since it has been in existence, has done nothing but promise salvation, and so far has not brought mankind even within hailing distance of it.

❖ ❖

Reliance on the future can be as much an escape from present responsibility as absorption in the past.

Salvation based on utopianism is as sterile as that which is based on other-worldliness.

❖ ❖

Salvation means to a person or a people being rescued from drowning in a sea of futility and meaninglessness.

❖ ❖

The Gaon of Vilna remarked, "I am surprised at the Almighty that He should have deemed it necessary to promise heavenly reward for the study of Torah. Is not the great delight which its study affords enough of a reward?"

❖ ❖

Heaven is that part of earth where one feels at home.

❖ ❖

Men have come to have religion not as a result of their quest for God but of their quest for salvation.

Having arrived at an idea of salvation, they fashion their idea of God in its image.

❖ ❖

The traditional heaven is not only an astronomical fiction but also a psychological absurdity.

It assumes that bliss is a destination instead of an expedition.

❖ ❖

When we do as we wish, we seldom get what we want.

❖ ❖

To be a complete person one has to be part of something super-personal.

❖ ❖

Salvation is durable happiness.
God is the Power that makes for salvation.

❖ ❖

Men will never achieve the promise of life so long as the only thing that unites them is the fear of death.

❖ ❖

To discover the way to salvation, we must have a philosophy of salvation.

❖ ❖

Whether we are saved or damned has nothing to do with the church, race, or people we belong to.

All who are educable are capable of salvation; all who are uneducable are damned.

❖ ❖

Some outstanding non-Jewish theologians are intent at present upon proving that human beings cannot achieve moral or spiritual perfection.

There are far more pressing problems to which they might devote their energies.

One of them within their jurisdiction is the following: how to prevent religion from being the divisive influence that it is at present.

As for the problem of perfection, we can afford to wait with crossing that bridge till we get to it.

The need for salvation, like the need for religion to which it gives rise, outlives all the mistaken notions about it.

When philosophers speak of God, insofar as what they say makes sense, they really speak of salvation.

The secularists look to security to give them salvation.

The religionists look to salvation to give them security.

If the religionists seem absurd in promising us *pie in heaven,* the secularists are no less absurd in trying to make us believe that pie *is* heaven.

A helpful glossary:

Hunger is physical or mental discomfort due to lack of necessary nourishment.

Pleasure is the feeling that accompanies satisfaction of hunger.

Happiness is pleasure without regrets.

Once we understand that by divinity we mean whatever makes for man's salvation or perfection, we might learn to see our basic human needs *sub specie divinitatis* (under the aspect of divinity).

Holiness is the quality which any being, person, object, event or situation possesses by reason of what it contributes to the fulfillment of man's destiny, or to the attainment of his salvation.

The sense of responsibility is the window through which man can look out on the cosmos and there discern God as the Power that makes for salvation.

You can always tell a demagogue by the way he makes readiness to die for a cause the criterion of its worthwhileness.

Not so our Torah. When it wants to command obedience to God's laws, it does so on the ground that "If a man do them he shall live by them." To which the Rabbis significantly add: "And not that they should be a means to death."

Someone said: "The average citizen's curiosity about water ends at the bathroom faucet. We know little about precipitation and run-off, the mysterious creep and flow of underground water and the as yet imperfect social instruments through which a unified governance of shared water must be attained."

Likewise the average Jew's curiosity about religion ends at *Kaddish* and *Kashrut*. We know little about what it is that gives man no rest, the mysterious forces that impel him to become human, and the imperfect social agencies, like churches and synagogues, through which a unified mankind has to be achieved, if man is ever to achieve salvation.

The religions and philosophies which preach detachment as a method of salvation seem to act on the principle that the surest way to cure a headache is to cut off the head.

Mankind will not be saved until involvement rather than detachment becomes the method of salvation.

Otherworldliness has been correctly defined as the assumption that "anything that makes this world more attractive makes the next world less attractive."

❖ ❖

To know how to go about making a religion into what it ought to be we must have a real understanding of what goes into the making of a religion.

❖ ❖

Don't merely expect to find or to believe that life is worthwhile; make it worthwhile.

Don't merely see life whole; make it whole.

❖ ❖

Church membership is viewed as life insurance for the next world. Like those who sell life insurance for this world, the minister works on the principle that life insurance is good for everyone, but he does not waste time with those who cannot afford it.

❖ ❖

Being important to someone, being needed by someone—that is fulfillment or salvation.

4. *Faith*

To love God is to refuse to let oneself be depressed by the world.

❖ ❖

There should be as much need for proving the compatibility of reason with faith, as for proving the compatibility of the compass, used in directing the boat's course, with the engine which generates the power that propels the boat.

A servant of God is a master of circumstances.

❖ ❖

To preserve faith, we must demolish dogma.

❖ ❖

The meticulous observance of ritual is not always an evidence of religious faith; it is often a sign of holy terror.

❖ ❖

There are people who, for very opposite reasons, expect religion to be based on absurdity.

They are the existentialists, who want to think with their emotions, and the atheists, who want an excuse for not having to think at all about religion.

❖ ❖

Idolatry is for the most part due to the logical fallacy that the indispensable is sufficient.

❖ ❖

Many a faith that is incandescent in a vacuum burns out quickly in the atmosphere of action.

❖ ❖

Piety exposed to the public eye curdles like milk exposed to the sun.

❖ ❖

The difference between believing in God and not believing in Him is equal to the difference between believing that the present crisis of humanity is part of man's growing pains and believing that it is a prelude to his extinction.

❖ ❖

The atheist is the kind of person who would conclude, from Andersen's tale of "The Emperor's Clothes," that no emperor has any clothes on.

❖ ❖

God preferred being challenged by Job to being defended by Job's theologian friends.

Better an ounce of sincere doubt than a pound of conventional theodicy.

❖ ❖

The religious doubt of the truly pious is a prayer and an expression of faith.

❖ ❖

Wanted: Men and women to serve God.

Discouraged people need not apply; God cannot use them.

❖ ❖

The Chinese claim that, of white jade alone, there are a hundred colors.

Why, then, may there not be at least a hundred ways of believing in God?

❖ ❖

The rose has its thorn and the flower of faith its dogmatism.

❖ ❖

It is as possible to believe continuously in God as it is to stay continuously awake.

Perhaps this is why the Psalmist prayed: May I be vouchsafed, when I awake, to behold Thy presence.

❖ ❖

Many a former aid to faith has become an obstacle to it. One such aid was the assumption that rain was a reward for obedience to the will of God.

❖ ❖

The demand for a justification of God's ways is itself a justification of His ways.

❖ ❖

Rational faith is two-thirds responsibility and one-third reason.

Irrational faith is all responsibility and no reason.

Sophistication is one-third reason and two-thirds irresponsibility.

The sophisticate who grows tired of his irresponsibility often reverts to irrational faith, because he does not wish to encounter any reminder of his original self.

We cannot afford to wait with our health until we know the final truth about our bodies and minds.

Neither can we afford to wait with our ethical and spiritual health until we know the ultimate truth about the world and God.

There are some important uses to a leap of faith, provided it is not a leap into the dark.

When, for example, we open the Ark before taking out a Scroll of the Torah, we chant two verses. One, taken from the Pentateuch, reads, "Arise, O Lord, and let Thine enemies be scattered." The other is taken from Isaiah. It reads, "For out of Zion shall go forth the Law."

The distance in time between those two verses is at least 500 years.

To recite them with any kind of understanding requires quite a leap of faith, but it is certain, at least, to land one on one's feet.

To esteem faith above reason, or reason above faith, is like preferring the bow to the string or the string to the bow.

What the Psalmist had in mind when he asked: "Who may ascend unto the mount of the Lord?" was not a sudden leap of faith, but the plodding climb of intelligence accompanied by deeds.

It seldom occurs to the adherents of a religion to be as critical of the superstitions in it as they are of analogous superstitions in the religion of their neighbors. Why is that?

The following story in *Listening With the Third Ear* by T. Reik, contains the answer:

A little boy who was spending the night at his aunt's complained about the fact that she had turned out the light.

"What is the matter with you, Tommy?" asked his aunt. "You sleep in the dark at home, don't you?"

"Yes, Auntie," replied the boy, "but it is in my own dark!"

❖ ❖

Some people get religion when they are frightened out of their wits.

Their religion shows it.

❖ ❖

To have faith in men is to assume that what men have in common will prevail over what differentiates them.

❖ ❖

If I am to have my choice, I prefer a life of reason bounded by faith, to a life of faith bounded by reason.

❖ ❖

The problem of religion is not one of faith versus reason but one of faith *in* reason.

❖ ❖

The traditionalist assumes that only our distant ancestors had religious experience. All that we, their descendants, are supposed to do is to enjoy our ancestors' religious experience by proxy.

❖ ❖

It is incredible to what depths of credulity the most astute mind can sink.

❖ ❖

Faith in God means faith that the present nature of man is an improvement on what it was 10,000 years ago, and that it is inferior to what it is destined to be in time to come.

5. Philosophy

On the most reliable testimony of scholars, Machiavelli was no Machiavellian, nor Nietzsche a Nietzschian.

On his own testimony, Karl Marx was no Marxist.

Among us Jews, Philo, Maimonides, and Spinoza had similar fates. Each one would have refused to subscribe to all that his disciples asserted in his name.

Why is this so often the case?

Because the master, seeing life whole, stresses the part which men ignore or fail to see.

But the disciple is so enamored of the part stressed by his master that he declares it to be the whole.

A philosophy of life becomes dated as soon as people cease to be bothered by the questions to which it was an answer.

Elijah Gaon (the Gaon of Vilna) is quoted as having said of Maimonides: "The cursed philosophy led him astray." Yet the very opening sentence of his own commentary to the *Book of Proverbs* reads thus: "Everything has four causes: the material, the efficient, the formal and the final." Where did he get that idea if not from "the cursed philosophy"?

Why some theologians malign philosophy, without which they could not be theologians, is one of the mysteries which psychologists are at a loss to explain.

Experience without philosophy is blind.
Philosophy without experience is empty.

❖ ❖

A certain popular Catholic preacher has attacked pragmatism again and again. What, if not pragmatism, is Jesus' teaching that "the tree is known by its fruits," and St. James' statement that "faith without works is dead"?

❖ ❖

So much was John Dewey the reincarnation of Socrates that, like Socrates, he too was charged with being the corrupter of youth.

Thank God, neither the State nor the Church could force him to drink the hemlock.

❖ ❖

A pessimist is one who bites off more of the future than he can chew.

❖ ❖

A visionary is a person who assumes that people want what they need.

❖ ❖

Existentialism is a philosophy of life which bases its conception of human nature on what mankind has been outgrowing instead of on what it is groping towards and painfully trying to become.

That is why existentialism is a philosophy of despair and should be regarded as the product of sick minds.

❖ ❖

A philosophy is a mythology in which you believe; a mythology is a philosophy in which you do not believe.

❖ ❖

Existentialism that revels in the absurd is morbidity with a touch of mysticism.

❖ ❖

Existentialists would evidently subscribe to the schoolboy's definition of an abstract noun as the name of some thing that doesn't exist, like honor or truthfulness.
That's how wrong they are!

❖ ❖

When existentialism creeps into poetry, you get such wisdom as the following: "A poem does not and should not mean anything; it is something."

❖ ❖

All values and ideals, to be authentic, have to be both timeless and timely, both absolute and relative, both means and ends. The philosophers and theologians who have stressed one requirement at the expense of the other are largely responsible for the present intellectual and spiritual disorientation.

❖ ❖

The new fad, Zen, is only another of those Far Eastern mysticisms which promise release from being a slave to freedom or responsibility. If that does not make sense, who says that Zen makes sense?

❖ ❖

Neo-Orthodox Christians and their Jewish fellow-travelers seem to be a theological front for the pagan existentialist philosophy of irrationalism and death.
The Nazis, who loved to designate their system "education for death," should serve as a warning against flirting with anything that smacks of a philosophy of doom, no matter how decked out it is in the spangles of religion or of freedom.
Spinoza was a wiser teacher than either Kierkegaard or Sartre.

He taught that "the free man thinks of anything but death; his wisdom is not death, but the pondering of life."

Likewise the Torah: "This day I place before you life and death. Therefore, choose life."

❖ ❖

If we could separate the wheat from the chaff in what is known as existentialism, we might obtain a very significant and nourishing truth. That truth is that you cannot reason into existence anything that doesn't exist.

You cannot, for example, by mere logic convince a Jew who has not had a Jewish upbringing or Jewish affiliations that he ought to be loyal to Judaism.

The function of reason is to maintain and improve an *existing* good and to abolish an *existing* evil.

❖ ❖

It is not the function of reason to create something out of nothing.

That is what "rationalists" do not seem to be aware of, and what it is the business of "existentialists" to remind them of.

❖ ❖

Theologians, in trying to account for the existence of evil, used to argue that it was necessary as a challenge to bring out the good in man.

Whenever radicals wanted to ridicule religion they would point to that argument as an example of the kind of spurious reasoning religion uses.

Along comes Jean Paul Sartre, the arch-enemy of religion, and plagiarizes that same kind of reasoning to make out a case for his existentialism.

"When I bring tolerance among my fellow-men," he says, "I have forcibly hurled them into a tolerant world. In doing so I have in principle taken away their free capacity for courage, for resistance, for perserverance, for self-testing, which they would have had the opportunity of developing in some world of intolerance."

That is not only perverse reasoning but also perverse morals.

There exist as many existentialisms as existentialists.

Sartre's kind of existentialism consists of licking one's chops when one feels nauseated. It raises *reductio ad nauseam* to a philosophy.

There is no disputing tastes.

The followers of Kierkegaard, whether Christian, Jewish or existentialist, have raised absurdity to a cult.

Kierkegaard himself did not originate the cult.

It goes back to Tertullian, one of the Fathers of the Church, who was fascinated most by the element of the absurd in the Christian conception of God, and declared: "I believe it just because it is absurd."

Apparently we are here confronted with a characteristic human trait.

The ascetic tenses the muscles of his character to get a sense of moral strength.

The absurdist tenses the muscles of his faith to get a sense of spiritual strength.

All these tensions are forms of what Freud calls "instinctual renunciation."

An existentialist is said to be one for whom existence is prior to essence.

What is the difference between existence and essence?

Existence is money in the bank; essence is a treatise on money.

In the war of "ideas" the fuzzy ones have the better of it, because of the difficulty in aiming at them.

Before we can have a theology we must have a philosophy of life to counter 1) the epidemic of irrationalism which has invaded the intellectual world, 2) the epidemic of nihilism which is disintegrating moral responsibility, and 3) the epidemic of defeatism which is poisoning spirituality.

An inventor is one who makes two blades of grass grow where there was only one before.

A philosopher is one who discovers two problems where other people thought there was only one.

Existentialism is fundamentally based on a false theory of human nature, on treating as cold literal fact what the ancients said in moments of despair when they declared that "the nature of man's heart is evil from his youth."

Those who think that the main business of theology is answering the question of why there is such a thing as evil, act as though theology were an apology for God.

No one philosophy is right except the one which says "no one philosophy is right."

In what is known as a "triumph of misguided technology," the radio and record engineers succeeded in producing recordings of music that were "acoustically perfect—i.e., completely dead."

These recordings lacked the depth and resonance of the concert hall.

Only recently a way has been found of reintroducing into the recordings the life-giving resonance.

That suggests what's wrong with agnostic humanism.

It is a triumph of misguided thinking in that it omits the lifegiving depth and resonance which only the dimension of the cosmos can give it.

No wonder the "perfect" logic of agnostic humanism does not save it from being "completely dead."

Romanticism assumes that it is man's function to imitate nature.

Rationalism assumes that it is man's function to improve nature.

That is why the romanticists add the inequalities of status to those of nature and the rationalists try to equalize the inequalities of nature.

Philosophers hitherto have tried to understand the world; the point, however, is to change it.

John Dewey conceived philosophy as a guide to change, as a constant criticism of culture from within, in response to its problems. He therefore thought of philosophy itself in terms of education, personal growth and transition in social change.

People who treat "pragmatic" as a dirty word, because it is supposed to deny the power of ideas, forget that so consistent a pragmatist as John Dewey maintained that ideas are the most practical things in the world.

It's not the concreteness or abstractness of an idea that matters. Once you start to operate with it you will find plenty of occasions to be emotional about it.

6. *Reason and Anti-Reason*

Freedom of thought has less to fear from the authority of reason than from the reasoning of authority.

The present wave of religious reaction, under the guise of existentialism and Neo-Orthodoxy, is only another manifestation of the principle that things must get worse before they get better.

Since rationalism cannot cure unhappiness, selfishness or demonism, it ends up by being blamed for them.

Intelligence is the awareness of the true relationship of means to ends.

It takes real intelligence to rate character above intelligence.

Tagore criticized Gandhi's policy of non-cooperation as being merely negative.

Gandhi, replying to Tagore's criticism, said that "Tagore's whole soul seems to rebel against the negative commandments of religion."

Further, he said, "non-cooperation with evil is as much a duty as cooperation with good.... Neti (not this) was the best description the authors of the Upanishads were able to find for Brahma."

Perhaps the Torah is not altogether wrong in having 365 "Dont's" as compared with 248 "Do's."

The ancient way of declaring absolute and authoritative whatever conformed with men's wishes or prejudices was to say that it was the will of God.

The modern way is to say that it is a law of nature.

A sense of proportion makes for common sense.

Sensitiveness to disproportion makes either for righteous indignation or for a sense of humor.

Righteous indignation without a sense of humor is only irritating.

A sense of humor without righteous indignation is only entertaining.

The difference between hallucination and reality is that in the first the dream masters us, while in the second we master the dream.

Wisdom is reason which, knowing its own limitations, cooperates with imaginative insight.

Belief in supernatural revelation as making good the inadequacies of reason seems to put a premium on ignorance.

The philosopher thinks in syllogisms, the moralist in pictures, the scientist in X-ray pictures.

The only way to develop reliable foresight is to cultivate clear-eyed hindsight.

According to Thomas Aquinas, reason is "hampered by the activity of the senses."

That is like saying that fire is hampered by its fuel—though that too can happen.

❖ ❖

We cannot save from irrelevance an idea that has become obsolete merely by declaring it absolute.

❖ ❖

The one thing the skeptic does not doubt is the validity of his skepticism.

❖ ❖

In trying to rescue reason from bondage to religion and science, we do not need to make them in turn its bondsmen.

Past experience can point to their having suffered starvation when left entirely to the mercy of reason.

❖ ❖

The most troublesome ghosts are ghosts of dead ideas; they refuse to be laid, and they refuse to let live.

❖ ❖

Sophistry is the ability to shoehorn falsehood into truth, and vice into virtue.

❖ ❖

Rationalization is the tribute that irrationalism pays to reason.

❖ ❖

If we are taught what to think but not how to think, we end up by not thinking at all.

❖ ❖

The problem is not how to get people to think, but how to get them to think with brains instead of their adrenal glands.

Aristotle regarded the brain as a cooling off organ. He was not entirely wrong.

❖ ❖

The only way to overcome the inflexibility of the mind is to unlimber it, to cultivate the art of thinking.

Scholarship is a life-line, but thought gives us the ability to use it. The latter is needed in all our preaching and teaching.

It is important to regulate one's intellectual diet so as not to suffer from constipated mentality.

Superstition with a philosophy is more dangerous than rationalism without one.

Most people are sure they hear an oracle if they see froth at the mouth.

There is genuine miracle to the "miracle drugs," but none to miracle cures.

Preconceptions are like keys. They are necessary to unlock the mind to new experiences, but they are generally used to lock the mind.

The yearning for infallibility (of which the belief in it is a product) is an unmistakable evidence of intellectual and emotional immaturity.

Once upon a time, to be accounted an intellectual you had to scandalize religion.

Nowadays to be accounted a religionist you have to scandalize reason.

The search for truth is hampered by the universal tendency to treat as the last word what is really only the first word in any revelation or discovery.

If you are allergic to superstition, stay away from doctors of theology. You are better off the way you are.

❖ ❖

According to Henri Bergson, reason cannot be relied upon, because you can always "reason" with reason. He would rather have us rely on faith and intuition.

We should like to know, however, what it to assure us that faith and intuition are not merely fancy names for unreason and credulity?

❖ ❖

When the will to believe gets out of hand, it becomes the will to prove.

❖ ❖

An I.Q. may indicate how far a person can go—but not in what direction.

❖ ❖

Scientists were formerly wont to define superstition as ignorance of the causal nexus. Nowadays scientists say that belief in the causal nexus is superstition.

❖ ❖

Common sense is words; philosophy is words about words; semantics is words about words about words.

That does not mean that we can dispense with semantics.

It only means that the human mind has gotten to be a three-story affair. If you want to get to the top story you need these three staircases.

❖ ❖

At first man struggles to free himself from the tyranny of nature. That gives rise to tradition.

Then nature avenges itself by trying to free man from tradition.

This gives rise to schizophrenia, in which man is torn between tradition and nature.

❖ ❖

The term "will to believe" is not intended to suggest that when we are asked to believe anything which flagrantly contradicts reason, we should grit our teeth, swallow hard, tense our muscles and make our mind believe in it nevertheless.

The "will to believe" means that when we encounter a fact which we are unable to handle by means of our customary thought instruments, we should not deny or ignore that fact, but exert our minds to produce the thought instruments that are adequate for it.

❖ ❖

Having a sense of values, or knowing that one thing is better than another, is not enough.

That's merely being like the Shah of Persia who refused to see a horse race, on the grounds that he knew in advance that one horse is bound to get ahead of the rest.

We must be excited over the most important values, excited enough to bet on them.

❖ ❖

To prohibit freedom of thought is no more of a protection against dangerous ideas than to stop breathing is a protection against dangerous germs in the air.

❖ ❖

Those who are afraid that debunking may have a demoralizing effect apparently consider morals to be dependent on bunk.

❖ ❖

The most fatal of all isms is somnambulism.

❖ ❖

Father Taylor, a priest in Boston who converted some of the habitués of Boston's waterfront, said, "It would take as many of Emerson's sermons to convert a man as it would take quarts of skimmed milk to make him drunk."

If converting a man is like getting him drunk, might it not be safer to let him remain unconverted and sober?

That being the case, Emersonian skimmed milk is probably more wholesome than Father Taylor's intoxicating sermons.

❖ ❖

Many a viewpoint is only another name for a blind spot.

❖ ❖

When someone tells you that he is satisfied with nothing less than *absolute truths,* whether supernaturally revealed or metaphysically demonstrable, you can confidently tell he is reaching out for the moon.

Advise him to be satisfied with the perennial *values.*

Those are the values of truth, justice, freedom, love, and holiness which alone make human life worth while.

❖ ❖

By this time we have to come to expect a tidal wave of irrationalism in the wake of a war.

Such irrationalism belongs to the same family of experience as that in which a person who stumbles in the dark lets off steam by kicking a chair.

When philosophical and religious irrationalists try to justify their attitude, they blame reason for all of mankind's ills.

Instead of suspecting that those ills might be due to mankind's failure to make sufficient use of reason, they are sure those ills come from the modicum of reason to which men resort.

If those irrationalists were not beyond the reach of reason, we would ask them to tell us, in all honesty, whether the chances of peace would not be improved if all concerned were to act reasonably rather than work themselves up into a state of hysteria.

❖ ❖

Poor reason has slaved and sweated for the philosophers only to have her reputation blackened by some of them.

Ernst Mach said she was little more than a sublimated belch of the food we eat, for what man is depends on what he eats. (*"Man ist was man isst."*)

Watson said she was nothing more than a mechanical toy.

Freud declared her to be a stooge for the unconscious.

No amount of irrefutable evidence will convince those who do not trust their own minds.

Anyone who maintains that the human being is essentially irrational probably thinks he is making a rational statement.

He therefore cannot be human. Does he regard himself as superhuman?

A general rule or principle as rarely fits a particular case without qualification as a ready-to-wear garment fits an individual customer without some alteration.

When we speak of intangible values which make life worth living, we tend to forget that they are relationships among tangible things and inconceivable without them.

Even wireless transmission of electricity implies transmitting and receiving sets.

Those who allow their thinking to be short-circuited should not complain that the light of faith and reason has gone out of their lives.

The philosopher Kant helped the human mind to pull itself out of the swamp of skepticism into which it had been thrust by the philosopher Hume.

Kant did it by teaching the human mind to pull itself up by its own bootstraps.

❖ ❖

A habit of mind worth cultivating is to judge men and things by what they grow into rather than by what they outgrew.

❖ ❖

Redefinition is to an idea or concept what growth is to a tree. An idea or concept begins to die as soon as it ceases to be redefined.

❖ ❖

Scientific method has nothing to contribute either to wisdom or to morale.

Whatever humility and devotion to truth scientists display are but part of wisdom.

What courage and patience they display in carrying out their experiments are but part of morale.

❖ ❖

Accuracy of vision is useless, unless we have the right point of view.

Accuracy of reasoning is worthless, unless we start with correct premises.

❖ ❖

There is nothing so irrefutable as absolute ignorance.

❖ ❖

When we set forth in search of truth, we should be warned against being directed by the quest for absolute certainty, as a traveler in the desert is warned against being misled by mirages.

❖ ❖

According to Bertrand Russell, Aristotle's philosophy is the same as Plato's, with a mixture of common sense.

Which implies that to have good sense you have to mix common sense with uncommon sense.

❖ ❖

The sneezing caused by the dusting off of forgotten philosophers is no proof of their reinstatement in men's thinking.

※ ※

The fact that the bright side of the moon has some spots does not justify worrying what is on the other side of it.

Likewise the fact that there are flaws in our reasoning is no excuse for resorting to mysticism.

※ ※

It takes considerable sophistication to de-sophisticate ourselves.

※ ※

The mind unquestionably needs opiates from time to time to take it off its troubles.

But the question is: Must those opiates, however, always be such poisons as alcohol, gambling, lying movies, and superstitious religion?

※ ※

The discovery of the irrational and the weird in the human mentality is no reason why we should bring back the belief in witchcraft.

※ ※

Eleanor Roosevelt says we should "demand facts unvarnished by interpretations."

She might as well ask us to convey thoughts "unvarnished" by words.

All language is interpretation.

As long as we have to use language to express facts we inevitably "varnish" them with interpretation.

What we should learn to demand is an honest varnish, one that doesn't make steel look like wood.

※ ※

Doubt or skepticism is as essential to the mind as salt to the body.

In hot weather, when together with our perspiration we give off much salt, we are advised to replenish it by taking salt pills.

Likewise, when, as the result of heated debate over politics, economics or religion, all doubt concerning the validity of our ideas evaporates, it is advisable to replenish it through careful attention to what our opponents have to say.

❖ ❖

There is more hope from enlightened self-interest than from ignorant altruism.

There is more hope from tolerant skepticism than from bigoted faith.

❖ ❖

To discover the unknown we have to be able to discover the obvious and to question the axiomatic.

❖ ❖

Any irrational philosophy or religion seems to be a comfortable resting place for "tired radicals."

❖ ❖

A poet's or philosopher's estimate of life is as much more reliable than a scientist's as a guest's judgment of a feast is more reliable than the cook's.

❖ ❖

Semantics is a therapy recently discovered to cure language of the diseases of vagueness, ambiguity, equivocation, simulation, evasion, and the like.

These are the diseases that befog the mind, poison the emotion, and paralyze the will.

❖ ❖

It is part of present-day irrationalism to regard any jabberwocky that is printed in small magazines as a communication from the gods.

❖ ❖

"Modern is beautiful when styled to comfort," reads a sign in a show-window displaying furniture for the home.

"Ancient is spiritual when styled to reason" might well be the motto for the furnishings of the minds.

Because we are in the habit of talking about people vaulting imaginary hurdles, we confuse imagination with hallucination.

The truth is that imagination is a special dimension of the mind, whereas hallucination is merely an eclipse of the mind.

The senses need imagination to discover what was and what is.

The intelligence needs imagination to foresee what can be or might be.

The reason needs imagination to be assured that what ought to be can be.

To rely upon reason does not mean to ignore the irrational in man and his environment. On the contrary, it means recognizing the irrational for what it is, and withholding from the attempt to make it appear rational.

To avoid the Scylla of wishful thinking and the Charybdis of fearful thinking, we should learn to navigate the channel of sound thinking.

It is natural for the anti-intellectual to hate reason, since reason is against him.

The pessimist Swift said the mass of men was as little qualified for thinking as for flying.

Now that he has been proved wrong in the matter of flying, perhaps he will in time be proved wrong in the matter of thinking.

Reason will be fighting a losing battle as long as it gives the impression that it is satisfied to have imagination monopolize our emotions.

We should be as emotional in the defense of reason as are fanatical dogmatists in the defense of unreason.

❖ ❖

Much of ancient thinking went awry because of the mistaken antithesis between body and soul.

Likewise, much of contemporary thinking goes astray because of the mistaken antithesis between reason and emotion.

Reason is to emotion what the reins are to the horse.

A circus rider who doesn't mind having his neck broken can get along without reins.

Likewise one who wants religion for the sheer excitement of it and doesn't care what it may do to his mind or character can afford to dispense with reason.

❖ ❖

It is no doubt true that intellect is influenced by non-intellectual elements of the human personality—by needs, desires, interests and by the emotions associated with them.

But it takes intellect to recognize that fact.

❖ ❖

In olden days, anti-rationalists were content to say: "I believe because it is absurd."

Post-modern anti-rationalists go further. They say, "I enjoy, I am inspired, I am thrilled, because it is absurd."

❖ ❖

The transition from the unconscious to the conscious is like the experience of being born, and, like that experience, it is attended by fear and protest.

❖ ❖

Understanding "people" in their own terms calls for a leap of reason that can do the world infinitely greater good than any leap of faith.

❖ ❖

The philosopher disparages the non-rational; the psychologist disparages the rational; the religionist at times disparages the one and at times the other. How does man come off?

❖ ❖

Science does not destroy the belief in miracle. It merely transfers that belief from the supernatural to the natural.

❖ ❖

Why do people affirm man's irrationality with such jauntiness, as though they were proud of the fact that they are moved by their emotions and their hunches to accept the shoddy for the real, and to delude themselves and the world?

❖ ❖

Is not fear of emotion itself an emotion?

Why then regard the intellectual who is afraid of emotion as unemotional?

❖ ❖

It takes more than two-thirds of the mind to overrule the veto of the viscera.

❖ ❖

When in our thinking we are about to take a leap, how are we to know whether it is to be one of faith or gullibility, unless we are sure to land safely?

Such assurance can come only from sound thinking before we get to the point of having to leap.

❖ ❖

Organizing a mass of detailed facts into a rational pattern enables our limited minds to handle them. It is like packaging a mass of goods into neat packages which makes it possible to handle them without any difficulty.

❖ ❖

Who may ascend the mountain of the Lord and who may stand in His sanctuary?

"He who is clean of hands and pure of heart."

Thus sang the Psalmist.

Nowadays, we have to add, "and clear of head."

❖ ❖

Rationalization is the tribute pretense pays to truth.

❖ ❖

In case you try to think clearly and to define your terms accurately and some bark at you: "You are only splitting hairs," snap back at them; "What's wrong with splitting hairs, provided you split them horizontally, the way the barber does when he gives you a haircut?"

The one dominant illusion we must get rid of is that illusion is indispensable.

❖ ❖

Definition is as good for the soul as it is for the mind. Stated technically, definition is as important for values as it is for facts, for commitments as well as for knowledge.

❖ ❖

The "dimmer" is a contrivance by which the light in an electric lamp can be increased or diminished gradually (instead of having to be turned on full or extinguished completely). That is the kind of logical contrivance which most people need. It would prevent their minds from being of the all or nothing type.

❖ ❖

Reason is to feeling what rhythm is to music.

❖ ❖

Nowadays when unreason has become a religion it takes a great deal of courage to have faith in reason.

Which only goes to show, on the one hand, that reason is no less dependent on courage and faith than unreason, and, on the other, that there is nothing intrinsically virtuous about courage and faith as such.

The ultimate destiny of man depends upon what he throws his lot in with: reason or unreason.

❖ ❖

To think is to argue with oneself. Most people don't like to get into any arguments.

That is why they hate to think.

The less you think, the more likely you are to be classed with "right-thinking" people.

❖ ❖

Only those who think are likely to let think.

❖ ❖

Horse sense is generally no better than what it claims to be.

❖ ❖

The reason so many people prefer to have closed minds is that, with the many winds of doctrine, they find open minds too drafty.

❖ ❖

It takes as much courage to think clearly as it takes brains.

❖ ❖

Montesquieu possessed such powers of deduction that he could derive the right conclusion from the wrong facts.

Sophists are people who manage to draw the wrong conclusions from correct facts.

To make facts yield any but logically inevitable conclusions is to open the floodgates of unreason.

Rabbi Meir, one of the famous disciples of Rabbi Akiba, was so clever that "his colleagues could not fathom the depths of his mind, for he could declare the virtually unclean to be clean, and supply a plausible proof."

That very cleverness deprived his legal opinion of the authority enjoyed by the opinions of his colleagues.

❖ ❖

The great tragedy of Judaism is that it has lost its minds.

❖ ❖

Nowadays when unreason has become a religion it takes a great deal of courage to have faith in reason.

❖ ❖

What is rationalization?

It is a "book bar," or a set of handsomely bound volumes of great poetry which, when opened, are found to contain one's favorite liquors.

❖ ❖

The evolution of the intellect is reflected in the three successive embodiments of civilization: the cleric who bases his authority on revelation, the jurist who bases his authority on precedent, and the scientist who bases his authority on consequences.

❖ ❖

An ancient Rabbinic saying declares that "truth is God's seal." For anything to be divine it must have the stamp of authenticity.

❖ ❖

Long before people learned to reason they rationalized. To this very day they cannot get rid of the habit of rationalizing.

❖ ❖

When reason dawns it disperses the last shadows of animism.

❖ ❖

RELIGION

Reason has its stages.

At first it promises salvation through the knowledge of the ultimate meaning of life.

Then it promises power through the knowledge of how to manipulate the forces of nature.

Finally it promises mundane fulfillment through the knowledge of how to engage in the meaningful employment of life.

7. Mysticism

Mysticism, which is not merely a form of belated magic but a reaching out for reality in all its concreteness, denies the assumption of the philosophers that God is absolutely unknowable.

On the contrary, it insists upon our experiencing His reality as vividly as we do our own.

The truth is that our own personality is inexhaustible, and therefore can never be fully known.

Most modern attempts at fostering religious mysticism are like trying to skate on steam.

How is it that Kierkegaard's existentialism can serve as sanction both for orthodox mysticism and confirmed atheism?

The answer is that Kierkegaard assumed that nature was hostile to man and his purposes.

From that, orthodox mystics infer that only God who transcends nature can help man, while confirmed atheists conclude that if man doesn't help himself no one else will.

Mystic faith in God which defies reason ends in idolatry.

Mystic faith in people which defies experience ends in dictatorship.

❖ ❖

Jewish philosophy considers the gulf between the divine and the human to be unbridgeable.

Jewish mysticism, on the contrary, emphasizes the proximity of the human to the divine.

Thus the *Zohar,* the Bible of Jewish mysticism, makes so bold as to say: "God rules man; but the saint rules God, for the saint can annul God's decree."

❖ ❖

The test of genuine mysticism is that it communicate some coherent state of mind. Any other kind of mysticism is quackery.

❖ ❖

"Myth" was once a term to denote anything which was so intrinsically irrational as to be unbelievable.

Nowadays we use the term to denote anything which is believed in with such emotional intensity that there is no need of explaining it rationally.

❖ ❖

People who make a display of their skepticism by questioning the obvious, generally end up as mystics who are immune to common sense.

❖ ❖

The atmosphere of divinity schools has recently become incense-laden with neo-mysticism.

Now and then one gets a whiff of empiricist disinfectant.

Won't somebody open the stained-glass windows and let in the fresh air of common sense?

❖ ❖

Very few people can get along without myths about the past and illusions about the future.

A mystic is a person who, in his eagerness to confront reality, loses all sense of reality.

The fact that hunches and snap judgments are arrived at without great mental effort does not necessarily render them divine inspiration.

Mysticism belongs to the twilight region between magic and poetry. We philosophize with our brains and mysticize with our viscera.

The neo-mystics of our day are not even original in the arrogance they derive from their alleged encounter with the divine.

Thus Gershom G. Scholem points out that the *Merkabah* visionaries (the eighth century mystics) were filled with pride of heart in the mystical presence of God.

Would we trust ourselves to a car without brakes? That is why we cannot allow the mind to go off on a mystical binge.

The fundamental difference between rationalism and mysticism is that the one is an instrument of control, while the other functions only when the controls are off. You can drug yourself into mysticism, but not into rationalism. If a drug for rationalism is ever to be discovered, it will take some one else's reason to make you use it, never your own.

A hunch becomes an intuition. The intuition evolves into a revelation. The revelation is identified as an encounter with the divine. Such is the mystic's progress.

❖ ❖

The value of mysticism is that, like a broad promise, it is assuring. But when we are in trouble—and as human beings we always are in trouble—we need more than assurance. We need enlightenment. That is what mysticism cannot give.

❖ ❖

Criticizing mysticism is about as rewarding an experience as attacking a fog.

❖ ❖

Mysticism is very often like a comet in the sky of theology, trailing a tail of fiery verbiage.

❖ ❖

The sun is far too bright for us to gaze at with naked eyes. That does not mean that the clouds which are formed by it help us to see it any better.

Neither do the clouds of mystic verbiage help us to have an immediate experience of divinity.

❖ ❖

Vincent Ohearn, in *This House Against This House,* contrasted the oppressive atmosphere of India with the gaiety and charm of China.

Those who got into the plane at Bengal and got out at Schechuan would exclaim, "God, what a relief!"

The explanation he gave is that China had been continually rational and ethical, whereas India had been mystic and metaphysical.

This should be a warning to those of our people who have a yen for brooding mysticism and for the intricacies of metaphysical abstractions.

❖ ❖

Mysticism is a philosophy expressed in metaphors.

Thus the philosophic fact that God is the correlate of the best that man can and should be is expressed in Jewish mysticism in the form that not only is God necessary to man but also that man is necessary to God.

8. Chosen People

No nation or *ecclesia* should count on being the prima donna in any future world opera, or playing solo with any future world orchestra.

None is so guilty of the cardinal sin of pride as those who claim to be infallible.

None is so given to claiming infallibility as those who declare pride to be a cardinal sin.

There may be more roads than one to a mountain-top view.

There may be more than one civilization leading to universal peace.

There may be more than one religion enabling men to achieve salvation.

By assuming that one's group is the hub of the universe, one manages to indulge one's vanity and egotism without the least twinge of conscience.

The way to overcome the tendency to feel like a worm is not by pretending to feel immensely larger than life size.

The way for Jews to overcome their sense of inferiority is not by pretending that they are a chosen people.

To say that the doctrine that the Jewish People is God-chosen means that it is God-choosing, is like saying that the teaching that God made man in His image means that man made God in his image—which is exactly what those who don't believe in God affirm!

❖ ❖

Those who argue that being divinely chosen means not being privileged but bearing responsibility, forget that being entrusted with responsibility is itself the highest privilege.

❖ ❖

The problem of how to spare an adopted child the shock which comes with learning the truth about its parentage was met by an ingenious mother in the following way.

"You know, my dear," she said to her adopted daughter of seven, "you are a very lucky girl. Other children are given to their parents who have to take them whether they want to or not. But you were selected by your father and me from a number of children, because we loved you."

All went well until about a year or so later when the mother became pregnant.

What was to happen to that ingenious explanation? And how was the adopted child to act toward the child that was about to come into the world?

Let those who insist on holding on to the doctrine of chosenness —be they Jews, Christians, or Moslems—ponder the question.

❖ ❖

Though we Jews are a people old in years, we are still a growing people.

An adolescent can't avoid becoming a man by wearing short pants.

The doctrine of chosenness means short pants for a mature people.

❖ ❖

"It is not without detriment to himself that a man cherishes the consciousness of being superior to his fellows, and the injury to his character is not least when he has best reason for his opinion."

That statement is not a random thought, but the carefully weighted opinion of George Foot Moore in what is the best work in any language on "normative Judaism."

Jews ought to apply that statement to the doctrine of the Chosen People.

Chanticleer thought that his crowing made the sun rise. Came a morning when the sun rose before he thought of crowing. Did he put an end to himself? No. He was satisfied with the role of announcing the dawn.

So why make a fuss when we discover that we are not chosen to bring the millenium? Is not the role of announcing the millenium in the face of universal chaos good enough?

To interpret divine chosenness as chosenness for service makes as much sense as being proud of one's humility.

The claim to chosenness which religious Jews assert is no longer asserted by them with that fervent faith in its literal truth which their forebears had.

It is no doubt intended to be nothing more than the expression of a self-conscious search for Jewish identity.

That, however, does not save it from being an irritant to sensitive Jews as well as to sensitive Gentiles.

Why then should Jews not find a happier designation of what they are than the traditional one of "Chosen People"?

Who but one that's gullible would ever base his opinion of an individual on what he thinks of himself?

Yet this is what traditional religion expects us to do. It expects us to accept uncritically whatever the religious group to which we belong thinks of itself. Actually a group should regard itself as less mature and less qualified to pass judgment on itself than an individual.

9. *Judaism and Christianity*

We Jews should be grateful to the Church for having preserved for us the writings of Philo, Josephus, the Apocrypha, and the Pseudepigrapha.

But the Church in turn is very much in debt to us Jews.

Besides being indebted to Judaism for its founder, and the teachings ascribed to him, Christianity is indebted to the Jewish people for having saved it from destruction at the hands of the Roman authorities.

"It was only the protection of the privileges which the Jewish *nation* had acquired in the Roman Empire," says the French Church historian Guignebert, "that the first Christian communities were able to spring up and take root without exciting the suspicion of the Roman authorities."

No wonder that, with such indebtedness to the Jewish people, Christendom is oppressed by a guilt feeling which finds its outlet in Jew-hatred.

This may be neither logical nor ethical, but it is perfectly psychological.

❖ ❖

Msgr. Fulton J. Sheen, in his book *Old Errors and New Labels*, argues as follows:

"A bad thought set loose is more dangerous than a wild man. There was once a time when a Christian society burned the thought ("burned the man who had the thought"—M.M.K.) in order to save society, and after all something can be said in favor of this practice. To kill one bad thought may mean salvation of ten thousand thinkers."

Now, suppose enough people came to the conclusion that the foregoing is *itself* a very bad thought, which is not at all improbable.

What would the logical conclusion be?

❖ ❖

The famous Cardinal Newman was probably apologizing for his having changed his Church when he said that "to live is to change: to be perfect is to have changed often."

Yet the Roman Catholic Church, to which he was converted, has as its motto: *"Semper idem"* (always the same).

How do the two things square?

As we say in Yiddish: *Bleibt a kashya* (Don't expect an answer!)

❖ ❖

"It is a familiar practice among churches," *The Christian Century* once editorialized, "to propose to end the sin of denominational division by having everybody else join the church which passes the resolution."

Has that not been the familiar practice of Christendom as a whole? Has it not proposed to end all religious differences by having all non-Christians join it?

❖ ❖

Universalists believe that all human beings, regardless of creed or race, will be saved.

There is said to be one Universalist to every fifty or sixty thousand Christians.

That is about the extent of his chance to be saved, according to his fellow Christians.

At times the Church acts as if Jesus had recommended that one should be as harmful as a serpent and as foolish as a dove.

A writer who is a disillusioned Marxist held up for emulation the neo-Thomist Jacques Maritain and the Protestant neo-Orthodox Karl Barth, and stated that there is "a need for a great theological reconstruction in the spirit of neo-Orthodoxy," by which he means Christian neo-Orthodoxy.

But why, necessarily, "in the spirit of neo-Orthodoxy?" Why not rather in the spirit of reason, which is certain to outlive all orthodoxies, both old and new?

In Christian religion, orthodox theology advocates the repeal of the element of sex in human nature; neo-orthodox theology, the element of power.

Despite some sensational conversions to Catholicism, the truth is that, while the roster of honorary membership in the organized religions is growing, the roster of active membership is decreasing.

The sickness with which sin is compared in Judaism is like a bad case of the grippe. The sickness with which sin is compared in Christianity is like a bad case of consumption. That explains why we Jews believe that sin is only acquired, whereas the Christians believe it is also inherited, or in the language of theology, "original."

The famous historian of Christian theology, Adolph Harnack, said: *"Wer eine Religion kennt, kennt alle."* (He who knows one religion knows all.)

The truth, however, is:

Wer nur eine Religion kennt, kennt keine. (He who knows only one religion knows none.)

❖ ❖

Somehow Christian writers and clergymen cannot get out of the habit of making religion synonymous with Christianity.

That is like making geography synonymous with the map of one's own country.

❖ ❖

The Christian poets and theologians, whose sadistic fantasies revelled in the description of the eternal torments to which the damned were subjected in hell, provided the blueprints and programs for the modern concentration camps.

❖ ❖

Christian neo-Orthodoxy is Pauline - Augustinian - Lutheran - Calvinist theology with "a new look."

❖ ❖

Judaism never has been, and is least of all nowadays, a resting place for tired minds and tired radicals.

❖ ❖

Christian neo-Orthodoxy may be said to aim at breaking man's will out of a mistaken deference to God's will.

The result is likely to be an increase in man's willfulness.

❖ ❖

It took a high Church dignitary like the late Archbishop of Canterbury to find it safe to write *Christianity and Social Order,* in which he gave a sympathetic study and defense of communism.

Such is the high cost of intellectual honesty.

❖ ❖

One form of assimilationism practiced by Jews is dressing up Christian theology to look Jewish.

Pouring the water of Jewish tradition on the old tea leaves of Christian theology doesn't brew Jewish theology.

Freeze the literalized form of the messianic belief as entertained by rural Jewry in the days of Herod, compound that with the neo-Platonic Midrash started by Philo the Jew—and you have the Christianity of the Church Fathers.

Take the Christianity of the Church Fathers, compound it with Rome's ambition to rule the world—and you have Roman Catholicism.

Jewish religion identifies God primarily as the redeemer from human bondage. That is because for Jewish religion man is essentially a free will, and only secondarily an immortal soul.

Christian religion identifies God primarily as the savior from death. That is because to Christian religion man is essentially an immortal soul, and only secondarily a free will.

Now that the Christian seminaries are renaming "homiletics" and calling it "preaching," perhaps the preachers will learn to call a spade a spade.

Burke, speaking of the American Revolution, said, "I do not know a method of drawing up an indictment against a whole people."

If he had studied the New Testament carefully he would have learned that method.

To labor, with the believing Christians, under the sense of having been born in sin, is to suffer from a persecution complex of cosmic dimensions, with God as the persecutor.

Some Jewish theologians and quasi-theologians still dwell within the lengthened shadow of Augustine.

In Jewish tradition, God himself always abides by the laws He commands. "Shall not the Judge of all earth act justly?" asks Abraham in wonderment.

In Christian tradition, Christ bids his followers to love their enemies. But as for his dealing with his own enemies, he declares "Whoever will disown me, I will disown him before my Father in heaven."

Religions differ not so much in what they teach as in the otherness of the means by which they teach.

The following will illustrate: According to Jewish teaching, the Ark of the Covenant bore its bearers. According to Thomas à Kempis, the cross bears those who bear it.

Jewish religion, with the Exodus as its focal point, raises history to the level of the divine.

Christian religion, with the cross as its focal point, raises mystery to the level of the divine.

Far more tragic than Christendom's massacre of millions of Jews is Christianity's need to caricature and to defame Judaism in order to vindicate that massacre.

Christianity cannot make restitution, as did West Germany, but the least it can do is to disavow its defamation of Judaism.

We have not yet grasped the significance of the fact that the first 1000 years of our history is part of the heritage of more than two thirds of mankind.

Traditional Judaism conceived its mission as that of saving the souls of its adherents for a share in the world to come. Traditional Christianity conceived its mission as saving the souls of its adherents from eternal perdition.

How does that jibe with the Christian assumption that it is a religion of love while Judaism is a religion of fear?

10. *Prayer*

Now that God is advertised in buses and subway cars together with wines, soaps and underwear, we shall have people going sermon-shopping, clergymen improving their salesmanship, and the children at services listening to sermons as they do to commercials.

Most people recite prayers they do not understand to a God they do not know. What passes for religion is not even superstition; it is sheer mummery.

Most people are resigned to the assumption that public worship is a periodic exercise in collective boredom.

Some people's notion of a house of worship is a place where, after parking your mind, you walk into your feelings.

The Christian clergy are having the same trouble as the rabbis to get the men to attend services.

This may be seen from the following ditty:
> "On the world's broad field of battle,
> In the bivouac of strife,
> You will find the Christian soldier
> Represented by his wife."

"Happy are they who *dwell* in Thy house," but not the transients who came for a day or two in the course of the year.

Thanksgiving implies appreciation of the benefits we enjoy.

It is an excellent antidote to the propensity to make unwarranted or neurotic demands upon the world.

Hence the devout recital of *Hamotzi* and *Birkat Hamazon* is good therapy.

The more you try to render worship esthetic the more anesthetic its effect is liable to be.

Religious worship, like everything else in life, should be three-dimensional: It should entertain, instruct and inspire; and it should maintain the proper balance among these three functions.

A true prayer is one the very utterance of which is partly its own fulfillment.

It is true that men worshiped God before they knew anything about religion, just as they sowed and reaped before they knew anything about the chemistry of the soil.

We have come to realize, however, that agriculture can be vastly improved through the study of soil chemistry.

The worship of God, too, would be more intelligent and fruitful, if we knew something about the nature of religion.

In the *Sefer Hasidim* there is a story of a shepherd who was too ignorant to recite the prescribed prayers. But the yearning to pray was so strong in him that he could not help making up his own prayer.

"O God," he prayed, "You surely know that if You had sheep which You would want me to take care of, I would do it for You without pay."

If that prayer could be translated into pastoral theology, we would have more and better religion in the world.

The reason why most people neglect prayer altogether, and the rest are afraid to tamper with its traditional form, is that whatever of it still survives is little more than reflex action.

It is incomparably easier to venerate the truth than to speak it, to admire righteousness than to practice it, to worship God than to obey Him.

We are told that to treat an itch according to the standards of modern medicine one has to know not only dermatology, but also allergy, neurology, etc.

Why, then, do people expect our spiritual physicians to cure the itch for pleasure, for money, for power, with a few incantations from the pulpit?

People whose religion begins and ends with worship and ritual practices are like soldiers forever maneuvering but never getting into action.

❖ ❖

In Jewish religion all authoritative prayers, whether of petition or for forgiveness, are bifocal, with God and Israel as their foci.

From this human standpoint they are we-centered and not I-centered.

They fulfill a spiritual function by infusing the ego with God-and-we-awareness.

❖ ❖

The most damaging use of religion is the ornamental, as when it is intended to confer respectability upon our social status. Perhaps no people is more expert in that use—or shall we say, abuse—of religion than the English.

Somerset Maugham tells us about his friend Augustus, who "was bored with religion," but who continued to have family prayers "as a social gesture becoming to a gentleman of ancient lineage."

❖ ❖

Worship, prayer or ritual can normally only relieve, express or enhance feeling: they cannot generate it where it is lacking.

Religious feelings can come only from a religious way of life. When they have to be worked up artificially through skillful manipulation of music, lights or dramatics, they are phony.

❖ ❖

There can be no question that good medical care is more likely to cure the sick than prayer.

Can we then dispense with prayer when one is sick?

No. We need prayer to remind us that good medical care is the way to obtain God's help for the sick, and to thank God for showing us that way.

But why bring God in? Why is not good medical care enough?

Because it cannot solve the problem of what a person should do with his health.

❖ ❖

Those who deem it presumptuous to make any changes in our traditional prayers, so as to have them conform with our present day conception of God and man, would do well to follow the spirit of our tradition instead of its letter.

Our sages went to great lengths in altering two important biblical texts which they introduced into the liturgy.

In the text which says of God that "He will not hold him guiltless who commits sin," the traditional liturgy deliberately omits the "not."

In the text which describes God as "He that maketh peace and createth evil," it deliberately replaces the word "evil" with "everything."

❖ ❖

The *Mishnah* lays down the rule that "Readers may not skip from place to place in the Pentateuch."

The reason given is that the rolling and unrolling of the scroll to find a new place was tedious for the congregation.

Why not use that as a precedent for rules with regard to the service as a whole, to prevent the congregation from finding it tedious or boring?

❖ ❖

The beginning of a moral conscience is a "factual" one.

How difficult it is for some people to acquire a "factual conscience" is proved by the doggedness with which they persist in affirming as real that which is non-existent, and as achievable that which is impossible.

It is more than a thousand years since the Jewish academies of Babylon have been on the map. Yet traditional Jews still pray every Sabbath for the welfare of the scholars who study there.

The State of Israel came into being as a democratic republic with a secularist Jew as its first president.

A thousand years from now there will probably still be Jews who will pray for the restoration of the sacrificial cult and for a scion of David to appear as the Messiah.

Hasidism's main contribution to Jewish life was its translation of Jewish religion into story, song, and dance.

The stories were about the *Tzadiķim,* the rabbis who exercised civil and religious authority over large numbers of *Hasidim.*

Though those were miracle stories, they gave new, vivid and dramatic expression to the spiritual and ethical aspects of Jewish religion.

Hasidic song and dance retrieved the intrinsic function of religious ritual.

We westernized Jews prefer to recite lugubriously in our seats: "O, come, let us exalt before the Lord; let us shout for joy to the rock of our salvation."

If we did so, some usher would quickly remind us that we are in a synagogue and not in the bleachers!

Those who make speed in *davvening* are experts in the automation of praying.

Solomon Schechter used the term "studying machines" to describe the students in the *Yeshivot* who competed with one another in study marathons. Those were the ones who introduced automation into the study of Torah.

Rhythm in self-expression is both effect and cause of deeply felt emotions.

The *Hasid* chanted and swayed to measure when he prayed.

Eighteen out of a hundred college girls in a certain sampling said they would rather be men than women.

So why should we be surprised that in the traditional liturgy the men are expected to thank God that they are not women?

In the traditional prayer book we thank God that He "has not made us like the nations of the different lands and has not placed us like the other families of the earth."

In our hearts we pray to God that He should make us part of the nations of the different lands and place us like other families of the earth.

That is the Jewish "dilemma."

Our sages rated the study of Torah above prayer.

They believed that we can derive much more good from hearing what God has to say to us than from having God know what we have to say to Him.

Perhaps we might achieve that same purpose by making silence part of our prayers.

Or, better still, by actually studying God's laws in nature and human life.

Thales of Miletus would thank the gods for having been created human not animal, a man and not a woman, a Greek and not a barbarian.

In our traditional ritual, the Jew thanks God for not having been created a Gentile, a slave, or a woman.

The time has come when we should be able to thank God for realizing the stupidity of thanking Him for the wrong things.

11. *Psychoanalysis and Religion*

Psychologists inform us that the first years of a person's life determine his character and happiness for the rest of his days. No wonder that the three fates, or Parcae of classic literature, look like nursemaids.

Many, if not most, of our psychic difficulties arise from the company we keep.

Psychoanalysis, in discovering that there is nothing original about sin, mistakenly thinks itself to be original in denying the reality of sin.

If you labor under a sense of guilt, you are a prospect for a psychiatrist.

If you indulge in a sense of complacency, the preacher will get after you.

Psychosomatics is a recent development in the art of healing. It reckons with the interaction of mind and body.

The next development will go a step further. It will recognize the interaction of society, mind, and body.

Then we shall have sociopsychosomatics.

When Plato wanted to find out what constituted a normal human being, he studied him in the magnified form of the state.

Nowadays, when a psychologist wants to find out what constitutes a normal human being, he has to study him in the exaggerated form of the neurotic.

Modern psychology has taught us to realize that we can know directly as little of our own minds as of our own bodies.

❖ ❖

The principle on which a good deal of mental healing seems to be based is that misery loves company. The cure consists in making the patient aware that his number is legion.

❖ ❖

A psychoanalyst is only a technician, who may understand everything about the mind except its ultimate nature and place in the universe.

Most psychoanalysts, however, think they are philosophers.

Without much ado, they reduce religion to an illusion, and morals dissolve at their touch.

There is nothing in their entire science to bridge the gap between the most intelligent act of the most intelligent animal and the miracle of the least significant word of a baby.

How then can they possibly undertake to handle concepts like God, justice, or love?

❖ ❖

Don't prick anyone's conscience—unless it's for a therapeutic inoculation.

In psychoanalysis there does not seem to be such a thing as "in the last analysis."

❖ ❖

Those who dabble in depth psychology begin to talk and write as though all surface psychology could be dispensed with.

Though the submarine has its uses, we still prefer to travel by ocean liner.

❖ ❖

How can you expect those who do not listen with more than half an ear to understand what those who listen with a third ear are talking about?

❖ ❖

While the behaviorist, J. B. Watson, was busy arguing away the existence of the conscious, Sigmund Freud was busy discovering the potency of the unconscious.

That Joshua Liebman's *Peace of Mind* and the self-help books that followed it have been for so long on non-fiction best-seller lists indicates that people are turning elsewhere than to the organized religions for the very thing on which religion claims to have a monopoly.

If we don't take care, psychoanalysis is likely to become a kind of religious cult.

It has already become the battlefield of warring sects, each claiming to have the exclusive key to the meaning of the Freudian gospel.

And, as in present-day Protestantism, appeals are being made for an ecumenical movement, to effect some unity among the contending sects.

The relations between religion and science will not improve through shoddy psychology or fake astronomy.

When religion learns to reckon with psychiatric truth, and psychiatry with religious truth, we shall have the whole truth.

The study of mental illness has yielded some very important information concerning the kind of God concept that is certain to aggravate such illness.

Thus Roland B. Gittelsohn, in a carefully conducted study, reports the following conclusions:

"God should be presented to mental patients as the inner Strength, Power or Resource which can assist the individual as he reaches toward recovery and health.

"The mystic element in religion must be minimized, if not altogether eliminated, in literature prepared for these patients."

Those conclusions forcibly prove that, from the standpoint of mental hygiene, it is helpful to present God as the Power that makes for salvation, and harmful to present God as the Power that makes for the sense of human homelessness. The latter is virtually what the Christian Neo-Orthodox and their Jewish fellow-travelers try to do.

There are two schools of psychology nowadays: one thinks religion is a disease, and the other thinks it is a cure.

St. Augustine taught that, in order to understand, we must believe.

The Rabbis taught that, in order to understand, we must act.

Which means that the Rabbis were better psychologists than St. Augustine.

Behaviorism, which sees nothing in human conduct but conditioned reflexes, is a form of reductionism which sees nothing in a diamond but carbon.

Self-consciousness, when normal, is self-transcendent; when abnormal, it is self-limiting and narrowing.

What is known as "racial memory" or "collective unconscious" is, according to Freud, the seat of folly.

According to Jung, it is the seat of wisdom.

Hence their differing attitudes toward religion. To Freud all religion is illusion; to Jung all religion is revelation. The problem: Who will analyze these analysts?

In the Middle Ages theologians had to come to terms with Aristotle. These days they have to come to terms with Freud.

Personality alteration which is achieved through psychoanalysis is repentance without benefit of clergy.

Personality alteration which is achieved through religion is repentance without benefit of psychoanalysts.

What more important function can religion have than to reassemble the psyche in each of us, which our anxieties would shatter into fragments?

Freud asked the right questions about religion, but gave the wrong answers.

He asked: Does religion keep the individual dependent, infantile and blindly obedient or does it emancipate the person, mature him and give him the capacity to face life with courage and productivity?

Suppose he had asked the same questions about educators. His answer would naturally have been: It all depends which education you are talking about. If you mean medieval education, of course it tried to keep the individual dependent, infantile and blindly obedient. But if you mean what some great educators have tried to make out of education, it certainly emancipates the person, etc.

He never would have said, "Education is an illusion."

Religion is in a thousand respects a form of education, labors under the same difficulties and has the same great potentialities as education.

Why then did he say religion was an illusion?

The answer is: He had never been psychoanalyzed.

To ascribe to the Judeo-Christian tradition the belief in the dignity of man is to impute to it a plagiarism either from Stoicism or from the so called "banalities" of eighteenth century rationalism.

According to St. Bernard men are but sacks of dung and food for worms.

We begin to appreciate the relativity of time when we realize the difference between God's greatness and man's greatness. God is great in that a thousand years are to Him as one day. Man is great when one day is as a thousand years.

A person never is. He either becomes, or wants to become, someone who could do what needs to be done.

The human being is essentially intellect, existentially emotion, and functionally will.

No idea is more responsible for having set the human mind on the wrong track than Aristotle's assumption that man's destination was contemplation.

III. ISRAEL

1. *Land and Nation*

Whence will come the leadership that will steer the Jews in the State of Israel safely through the turbulent waters between the Scylla of religious romanticism and bigotry, and the Charybdis of Marxist socialism and atheism?

The present condition of man is such that it is safer for the Jew in Israel to celebrate the festival of Sukkot with a gun and a grenade than with a *Lulav* and an *Etrog*.

Ronald Storrs, the first Governor of Jerusalem under the British mandate, was quite an antiquarian of scholarly attainment.

He had an idea that the old city of Jerusalem ought to be emptied of its inhabitants and made into a museum of the three world religions. He wanted to see it preserved as it was, with all its narrow, steep, and dark alleys and its ancient stone houses untouched by anything modern.

The anti-religionist Jews in the State of Israel concur with the extreme Orthodox in opposing all attempts to tamper with traditional religious ritual. They do not want to see a jot or tittle in it changed because they would like to have the traditional ritual preserved as a museum piece.

It is amazing what strange bedfellows the museological interest can bring together.

Indeed, much of what people judge to be a religious revival is fundamentally only a variation of what sends the ladies in the summer colonies shopping for antiques.

When will the Messiah really come, or when will the Messianic era begin?

When Reform and Conservative Rabbis are allowed to officiate in Israel, and when the Chief Rabbi of Israel is permitted to visit the institutions that train them in the United States.

The Government of Israel has been experimenting with a new emulsion: democracy with theocracy.

It would work if both democrats and theocrats were amenable to reason.

"Happy is the people whose annals are tiresome," said Carlyle.

By this time Israel could well stand having her annals become slightly tiresome.

The main religious concept which is Zionism's contribution to Judaism is a new formulation of the principle of faith.

That formulation is *af al pi ken velamrot hakol,* "nevertheless and in spite of everything."

It is highly important to watch the convalescent.

The reconditioning of the sick and disabled ends only when the patient is completely readjusted.

That is why we are not relaxed in our efforts for the State of Israel.

In Israel there is a large output of Hebrew books dealing with the history, life, and culture of the Arabs.

There is little dealing with American Jewry.

Which only proves that a near neighbor, however troublesome, counts for more than a distant brother, however helpful.

Let us not permit the State of Israel to become the opiate of Diaspora Jewry.

Who knows but that we Jews are being shaped by the Power that makes for salvation into a "spearhead of the creativity" that will save mankind from its impending doom?

What the Crown is to England, that the Land of Israel is to the Jewish People—"an unsurpassed symbol both of continuity and unity."

"I can conceive of nothing more lamentable than a petty Jewish state," once pontificated Lessing Rosenwald, the leader of the American Council for Judaism.

Discussing Albania's appearance years ago as a witness against Italy at the Paris Peace Conference, Anne O'Hare McCormick noted the extraordinary fact that the Albanian nation, which counts less than a million souls, has managed to preserve its own language, customs, and individual character through the vicissitudes and conquests of two thousand years.

But you will say "What more than a little satellite can an Albania or Israel be?"

Why be snooty about satellites? The earth is a small satellite to a mediocre star in the infinite spaces. That doesn't prevent man from thinking himself the center of the universe.

Winston Churchill, in his book, *The Gathering Storm,* tells us why he preferred to become the Lord Admiral of the Navy to being a Minister without Portfolio.

"It is easier," he says, "to give directions than advice, and more agreeable to have a right to act even in a limited sphere than the privilege to talk at large."

That, in a nutshell, explains why Jews prefer having a State of Israel to being roving missionaries.

When asked for the explanation of the miracle enacted in the State of Israel during the first year of its existence, the Jews there answer that the matter was as simple as *Aleph Bet.*

Aleph Bet is the abbreviation of *Ain B'rera* (there is no choice).

Which reminds us of the old legend about the toad.

The toad had fallen into a hole from which no amount of scrambling seemed to make it possible for him to crawl out.

His friends stood around giving him advice and encouragement. Seeing that they could not help him, they departed with a sigh.

Next day he was seen hopping along the road as of old.

"We thought you wouldn't be able to get out of the hole," they cried out in surprise.

"That's what I thought, too, but a truck came along and I simply had to get out." *Ain B'rera.*

Perhaps this is the meaning of the oracle, "As I live, saith the Lord God, surely with a mighty hand . . . will I rule over you."

The State of Israel does not coincide with the Jewish people; neither is it coextensive with the whole of Judaism.

We Jews have to maintain our historic position that a state **is not the supreme form of human association.**

Only those who are actively united for the furtherance of universal freedom, justice and peace, whether they be few or many, constitute the supreme form of human association.

❖ ❖

Among the few suggestive ideas in Toynbee's much touted, *A Study of History,* is the one that goes by the term "withdrawal and return."

It refers to the part played in history by the tendency of some moral or religious genius to withdraw from his accustomed surroundings, and, after having spent some time in isolation replenishing his inner resources, to return to his world and give it the benefit of his augmented powers.

If Toynbee were not blinded by his Christian prejudice against the Jews, he would have seen in the contemporary miracle which the Jews are enacting these days a large-scale illustration of the process of "withdrawal and return."

❖ ❖

The spirit of the Jewish youth in Israel shines out from the following dialogue between a man of sixty and a youth of eighteen, during the War of Independence.

Said the man to the youth: "Do you believe we shall overcome our enemies?"

"I may not live to see it," replied the youth, "but you will."

❖ ❖

Adobe bricks that were dried and baked two hundred years ago were found to contain seeds of plants.

When the bricks were broken up and soaked in water the seeds began to sprout again.

Should we doubt then that, with the breaking up of the two thousand year old *Galut,* the seeds of Israel's creativity are again coming to life?

❖ ❖

When Jews are shocked by the behavior of the religious fanatics who bring disgrace to the State of Israel, let us remember that Dwight Moody said: "I have never met a man who has given me as much trouble as myself." The same applies to peoples.

We should like to suggest to Israelis not to try to persuade American Jews to migrate to Israel on the ground that "it can happen here." That is as foolish as urging people to build bomb shelters against an atom bomb attack.

Zangwill coined the term "Torah-latry" to denote the worship of the letter of Jewish tradition. A worshiper of that kind recently declared that Israel should be a Torahcracy.

In such Torahcracy, democracy had as much chance as a snowball in an atomic reactor.

The establishment of Israel should not mean an addition of one more nation to the roster of the world's trouble makers, big or little.

It should serve as a retroactive rationale for all that the Jewish people has hoped for throughout the thirty-three centuries of its checkered career.

An even greater miracle than the rapid growth of the Jewish population of the State of Israel would be a correspondingly rapid growth in political and spiritual maturity.

Such maturity is possible only to a state whose citizens know how to render personal independence and national prestige mutually compatible.

Theocracy is as much in place in a modern state as a model T is on a super-highway.

Nothing develops personality like success in a task.

Nothing, therefore, is so essential to Jewish personality as success in the task of establishing security in the State of Israel.

❖ ❖

The Jews in Israel, despite all they have to cope with, have a heartening effect on the Jews who come to visit them.

They act like those rare patients who cheer up their visitors.

❖ ❖

Among the achievements of Zionism should be included the fact that it has taught Jews the art of creative leadership, thus saving them from the frustrations of philanthropic, and the dull routine of administrative, leadership.

❖ ❖

Resh Lakish, a rabbi of 3rd century Eretz Yisrael, would occasionally burst out laughing.

But he learned to restrain himself after he heard his colleague Rabbi Johanan quoting an ancient authority to the effect that so long as we Jews are a homeless people, it is not right for us to regale ourselves.

The inference, of course, is that in the coming age, as Zion is rebuilt, "our mouth will be filled with laughter" (Ps. 126).

❖ ❖

"Many a man became a genius through the girl he didn't get, and only a Privy Councilor through the girl he got," says Kierkegaard.

Is the Jewish people to have a similar fate?

So long as we were without a state, we aspired to spiritual greatness; now that we have one, are we to be satisfied with national littleness?

❖ ❖

Israeli Jews are on the stage. Diaspora Jews are in the orchestra.

That explains why Diaspora Jews have so much more knowledge about Israeli Jews, than Israeli Jews have of Diaspora Jews.

❖ ❖

John Hersey described the shame of the pastor of the Hiroshima Methodist Church, who was miraculously unhurt when the atomic bomb exploded there. Everywhere he apologized to the wounded, "Excuse me for having no burden like yours."

That is the way we American Jews ought to feel when we recall the six million Jews martyred in Europe and the ongoing task of the Jews in Israel, building with one hand and defending themselves with the other. We ought to say to them, "Excuse me for having no burden like yours."

❖ ❖

While our Prophets ought undoubtedly to be revered for having aroused the ethical impulse in man, they cannot always be credited with having channeled it wisely.

Thus the same Prophet who says, "I, the Lord, love justice; I hate robbery with iniquity" (Isaiah 61:8), promises the Jews who are to return from captivity, "Strangers shall stand and feed your flocks, and aliens shall be your plowmen and your vine-dressers" (61:5).

How much more ethical is the economy of modern Israel, which has repudiated that promise and stresses the value of self-labor!

If Israeli Jews want American Jews to settle in Israel they have to create for Israel not only absorptive capacity but also attractive capacity. That involves making the Jewish community of Israel worthy of being the center of world Jewry.

❖ ❖

Eretz Yisrael should not be expected to be a hothouse of moral virtue where perfect human beings are grown.

It might well be a garden of human character which requires constant cultivation and weeding.

Eretz Yisrael is to the Jewish People what the skin is to the human body.

As the skin joins the human body to its environment so does Eretz Yisrael join the Jewish People to the rest of the world.

2. *Jewish Peoplehood*

The character of a people derives, in large part, from the circumstances under which it is born.

The People of Israel, having been born in redemption from bondage, has the love of freedom and the sense of human dignity deeply engraved in its consciousness.

Our future as a people depends upon our ability to transform Judaism from a fixated to a dynamic civilization.

In the struggle against assimilation, Jewish survivalists should be careful to choose the ground where they have a chance of winning.

We would advise them not to choose theology, which is all about God, but those ologies, like psychology, anthropology, and sociology, which are all about man.

Judaism is amenable to a variety of interpretations, but not to one which is false to the nature and history of the Jewish People.

Tradition can tell us who we are—but not what we should do.

What we should do depends on three things: who we are plus where we are and whither we want to go.

❖ ❖

"Everything ideal has its natural basis; everything natural has its ideal fulfillment," said Santayana.

That is why Judaism must have the Jewish People as its basis; and that is why the Jewish People must find its fulfillment in Judaism.

❖ ❖

So long as we Jews do not reconstitute ourselves into a People with a status that reckons with the realities of the modern world, we shall continue as a kinship nationality. Such a status is an anachronism in a present-day democratic society.

To persist in that status is to be a living fossil.

To fail to achieve a tenable status is to become a dead fossil.

❖ ❖

If we read with understanding the prayers we recite in a Jewish service, we would discover that they are meant to be a means of getting us to identify ourselves with the Jewish People, and of arousing in us a passionate yearning that our People rise to great spiritual heights.

❖ ❖

Horatio Greenough, a distinguished American architect of the early 19th century, said that the American builder, by a truly philosophic investigation of ancient art, would learn from the Greeks to be American.

By the same token, the American citizen, by a careful study of biblical religion, would learn from the Jews to be American.

❖ ❖

We Jews are evolving into a new type of human society—a people, which, though scattered, is rendered one and indivisible through its spiritual nucleus in the land of its birth.

We are experimenting with a hitherto untried means of cohesion—the love elicited by a common tradition and a common fate.

It is sometimes thought that it takes the threat of hell-fire to keep a *church* together.

We want to prove that love—born of a common history and a common destiny—can keep a *people* together.

❖ ❖

One cannot be a Jew without active belonging to the Jewish People, even as one cannot be a soldier without belonging to an army.

❖ ❖

Destiny is all too often used as an alibi for drift.

❖ ❖

To be subject to a common lot is not the same as having a common destiny.

❖ ❖

The loyalty which a people elicits is due far less to the glories of its past than to those of its expected future.

❖ ❖

Those who object to making the survival of the Jewish People the motive of Jewish activity or ritual observance forget one thing: that to survive in the kind of world we have these days is itself an achievement that calls for the exercise of our highest powers.

❖ ❖

We already have what Sholom Aleichem designated as *"amkha"* (Thy People)—the unsophisticated Jewish masses.

We now also have "Israel"—the state which Zionism has helped to establish.

We are still in need of what our traditional liturgy speaks of as *"amkha Yisrael"*—the reality of the indivisible Jewish People, united by a common spiritual destiny.

❖ ❖

Jewish religion without Jewish People is like a rudder without a boat.

❖ ❖

If the American Council for Judaism had its way, the highest status to which the Jewish People should aspire would be a congregate body of furtive mice.

❖ ❖

No Jew should want to be counted as a Jew without counting as one.

❖ ❖

Rabbis and educators go at the problem of Judaism's future backward when they try to conserve the little of Jewish life that they can mobilize in the synagogue and the schools, but fail to make provision for the spiritual solidarity of the Jewish People.

They are like the engineers and promoters who, ignoring the need of vegetative cover at the water sheds, proceed to build great dams which, for lack of that cover at the headlands, are soon silted and rendered useless.

❖ ❖

There is nothing wrong with being a man or a people with a mission.

What's wrong is deciding for everyone else what the mission should be.

❖ ❖

However much we Jews may vaunt our mission to the Gentiles, an American Jew would have good reason to be satisfied with the Irish sense of ethnic self-respect, and with the Quaker feeling that religion must make an ethical difference in a person's life.

❖ ❖

To be reborn we have to live down having been long dead.

❖ ❖

It is the body rather than the mind that makes men want to live.

Likewise, it is the fact and feeling of belonging to the body of the Jewish People rather than a particular ideology that makes a Jew want to keep alive as a Jew.

❖ ❖

Part of the mystery of peoplehood is that we feel impelled to live for posterity, and that posterity will look to us for life's meaning.

❖ ❖

The future of Zionism depends upon how Zionism views the future of the Jewish People.

❖ ❖

The continuity of Judaism is in the continuing will of the Jewish People to live, and not in its conception of God, which merely reflects a reaction to the contemporary climate of opinion.

❖ ❖

We have been so busy living up to our promise to Peter Stuyvesant not to be a burden to our neighbors, that we have failed to do all that is needed to prevent our being a burden to ourselves.

❖ ❖

"Israel has given our People," said Ben Gurion, "the new Jew and the new man."

That is quite an overstatement.

Reduced to proper size to conform to literal fact, that statement should read as follows:

Israel has given our People the opportunity to produce the new Jew.

To make that opportunity good Israel should try to formulate the idea of the new man. Only then will the new Jew be the new man.

❖ ❖

A possible answer to the question "Who is a Jew?" may be: *Kol yisrael arevim zeh va-zeh*. In other words, all persons who come within the scope of the formula that Jews are responsible for one another as Jews.

The extent of that responsibility is determined not only by Jews but also by non-Jews.

❖ ❖

So important is a name which defines or gives status that nothing is so hopeless as nameless melancholy. The saddest fact about our existence as Jews is that it is nameless.

❖ ❖

"Happy Jewish worrier" describes the function of the American rabbi. There's plenty to worry about in the rabbinate—most of all whether there is a future and what kind of a future for Judaism in the world.

What should make him happy is the fact that even if he is frustrated in achieving his purpose, he can still find life worthwhile. That is entirely possible if his purpose is such as to be itself worthwhile, for by pursuing it the rabbi's own personality is bound to grow in knowledge, will power and enthusiasm for living.

❖ ❖

"No man can be a great writer without having a great philosophy . . . a high respect for values. His essential function is to raise life to the dignity of thought and this he does by giving it shape," writes André Maurois.

No man can serve the Jewish people without having a great philosophy . . . a high respect for moral and spiritual values. His essential function is to raise Jewish life—its peoplehood, culture, and religion to the dignity of thought and this is done by giving it shape, a land, a polity and institutions.

❖ ❖

Our problem is how to make Judaism safe for diversity as well as a source of uniformity.

3. *Jewish Denominationalism*

Unless we Jews learn, despite all our differences, to pull together, we are certain to pull apart what still remains of Jewish life.

Every one of the Jewish denominations is actually a coalition of sub-denominations.

❖ ❖

Jews diverge into different religious sects, to the detriment of Jewish religion, on the basis of a gradually diminishing "yarmulke," which is *on* the head.

Christians diverge into different religious denominations, to the detriment of Christian religion, on the basis of the same gradually dwindling "notion," which is *in* the head.

❖ ❖

One had to go outside New York City to see the kind of traffic lights that symbolize the three largest religious trends among us Jews.

The green light is an appropriate symbol for the Reform Movement in most matters involving traditional Jewish practice.

The red light, on the other hand, is the proper signal for Orthodoxy, which, on the whole, inhibits all attempts to introduce any changes in the traditional code.

The yellow light appears to be specially created to represent the hesitant and halting moves of the Conservative Movement. It is generally a transition signal; and one never knows whether to stand still or to go ahead.

❖ ❖

The Orthodox and Reform Movements in Judaism have each a clear purpose.

The Conservative Movement is in search of a purpose.

Organic Jewish community, undivided by differences of religion, or social status, is in search of a sponsor.

What can be more logical than that the Conservative Movement should sponsor organic community?

❖ ❖

The seeming permanence of the Reform congregations is due to their being constantly renewed by former members of Conservative congregations; of Conservative congregations by former members of Orthodox congregations; of Orthodox congregations by former members of traditionalist congregations.

They are very much like seafoam which, though actually dissolving, is ever present, because it is always being renewed from below.

❖ ❖

Many a Conservative Jew becomes a Reform Jew at the drop of a hat.

❖ ❖

Judaism will benefit more from honest criticism than from partisan advertising.

❖ ❖

When your train moves at a different speed from that of the one on the adjoining track, you are under the illusion that your train is moving in the opposite direction.

So long as Conservative Judaism is merely moving more slowly in the same direction as classical Reform, or faster in the same direction as Neo-Orthodoxy, it gives the illusion of moving in the opposite direction.

❖ ❖

If we want to solve the problem of diversity in Judaism, we must have Universities of Judaism.

❖ ❖

Many Conservatives have taken over from Reconstructionism the conception of Judaism as an evolving religious civilization.

The difference between them and us turns upon the definition of evolving.

They limit it to inevitable and automatic development.

We stress "evolving" as urgent and imperative for our day—deliberately planned reconstruction.

Why do we Jews have three kinds of synagogues, Orthodox, Reform, and Conservative?

Perhaps the answer may be found in a story Bennett Cerf told not long ago.

It is about a man who had risen from poverty to riches and who had acquired a sumptuous estate.

The guests whom he had invited to view his estate were surprised to find three swimming pools. Two were filled and one was empty.

He explained that one had warm water and another cold water. But why was one empty?

"You'd be surprised," he replied, "how many of my guests can't swim."

Orthodoxy can't always be wrong. Even a clock which has stopped registers correct time twice a day.

To divide Judaism is to help its enemies to conquer it.

The House of Israel cannot afford to be one-tenth unionist and nine-tenths secessionist.

Jewish religion without the Jewish People is like a skylight without the house.

The Jewish People without Jewish religion is like a house without windows.

The traditionalists prefer stained-glass windows; the Reconstructionists want the windows to be transparent.

When Orthodoxy no longer stands still and begins to mark time, it becomes Conservatism. When Conservatism stops marking time and begins to march, it has the choice of either taking the course that leads to a dead end, or following the path that leads to the fulfillment of Israel's destiny.

Disraeli wrote in *Coningsby*: "I observe a party in the state whose rule it is to consent to no change, until it is clamorously called for, and then instantly to yield: but these are concessionary, not conservative principles."

That sums up in a nutshell what's wrong with the principle of "Catholic Israel" as a formula for Conservative Judaism.

What "Catholic Israel" advocates is a concessionary, not a Conservative Judaism.

Some outstanding Orthodox rabbis refuse to deliver lectures in Conservative and Reform synagogues.

They do not mind, however, delivering their lectures in the vestry rooms of centers which belong to these synagogues.

That might justifiably lead many people to infer that the center offers more of a common ground for Jewish cultural unity than the Synagogue.

Which does not augur so well for the Synagogue.

Among us Jews there are interdenominational groups that upset all calculations and confuse all issues: the non-observant Orthodox, the non-conforming Conservatives, the non-progressive Reformers, and the secularists who love to hear a good *hazzan*.

The Conservative movement, except for the Reconstructionist wing in it, is "tired" of Orthodoxy and is "afeared" of non-Orthodoxy.

The Conservative movement in Judaism would fare much better if it were not inhibited by a residual Orthodoxy.

At a recent rabbinical convention the criterion of rabbinic affiliation was defined as follows:

An Orthodox rabbi always wears his skull-cap.

A Reform rabbi never wears a skull-cap.

A Conservative rabbi keeps his in his pocket always ready for use.

Orthodoxy views religion as a solution in search of a problem.

We Jews are a people with a common fate in search of a common faith.

Our problem is, therefore, how to carve out a common faith from our common fate.

Our three large religious groups, the Orthodox, Conservative and Reform, are intersected by three other groups: those who believe, those who don't believe and those who make believe.

We are told that a person who has had his arm amputated but who has retained a nerve stump leading to the fingers will imagine that the pain which accompanies the pricking of that nerve stump is seated in the fingers.

Likewise many a Jew who has cut himself off from his Jewish people continues to suffer the pain which Jew-hatred inflicts as though he were still part of the Jewish People.

❖ ❖

When the different religious denominations in Judaism treat one another as rivals and competitors, they are battling on the edge of a precipice.

❖ ❖

The average Conservative Jew is Orthodox by nostalgia, Reform by practice and Conservative by affiliation.

❖ ❖

Jews who quarrel about Orthodoxy, Conservatism and Reform nowadays, when the very survival of Judaism is threatened by cultural and religious assimilation, are like two people who become embroiled in a quarrel about issues they deem highly important when suddenly a hurricane breaks out and threatens to destroy both of them. If they had any sense, they would help one another to do something to counteract the danger of assimilation which strikes all religious groups alike. That might involve finding compromises.

4. *Organic Community*

Why would it be so much easier to live and function as a Jew in an organic community than within the confines of an individual congregation?

Because it is easier to swim in the ocean than in a bathtub.

❖ ❖

The essence of a democracy, according to Ernest Barker, consists in "enlisting the affective thought of the whole community in the operation of discussion."

This explains why democracy in Jewish life and religion is the only guarantee of their future in this country.

❖ ❖

In a changing world, the leaders of a passing order usually waste their energies fighting the emerging order instead of using them to qualify for the new type of leadership.

In ancient times the Sadducee leaders, whose way of life was centered in the Temple, wasted their energies fighting the way of life centered in Torah.

Nowadays, the old Rav, who functioned in a segregated Jewish life, is still combating the westernization of that life.

And, lately, the rabbis who minister to congregations try foolishly to stop the development of the Jewish communal centers, instead of reorganizing the entire structure of American Jewish life, so as to find room in it for as many types of Jewish fellowship as conditions demand.

❖ ❖

Expecting the synagogue by itself to save American Jewry from disintegration is like hanging on desperately to the handrail of a falling elevator.

❖ ❖

The only alternative for us Jews as a people to being a dead fossil is being a living organism.

We cannot choose to be a living fossil.

❖ ❖

In treating a major burn, the physician is expected to treat not only the burn but the patient as a whole.

In his concern for the burned area the physician must not overlook the general treatment of the patient.

The Jewish people has suffered a major burn during the last War.

In our eagerness to heal that part of it which is now a raw and gaping wound, let us not overlook the general body of our people everywhere, and let us try to guard it against all possible inner complications.

❖ ❖

If American Jews wish to replace drift with mastery they have to create a direction-finding instrument—a University of Judaism—, and a direction-holding instrument—an American Jewish Community.

❖ ❖

American Jewry lives from hand to mouth. Its public causes and communal institutions have no reserves to fall back on.

And it lives from mouth to hand. Instead of building up permanent sources of revenue, it relies, for meeting its budget, upon the oratory of its campaigners.

❖ ❖

Many Jews are psychologically conditioned against communal unity.

They seem to interpret God's promise to Abraham that his descendants would be like the sand of the sea as prophesying their incapacity to fuse.

❖ ❖

Now that we are coming to realize the advantages of socialized medicine, we might discover the advantage of socialized religion.

Instead of each congregation and its rabbi conducting religious and educational activities on the private enterprise plan in the usual unsavory spirit of competition, those activities would be far more fruitful spiritually if taken over by an inclusive organic community.

❖ ❖

If Jews will not establish organic community for the conservation and enhancement of Judaism, Judaism will go into receivership, to be auctioned off to the entrepreneurs of provisional synagogues, to marrying and burying "reverends," to rabbinical and lay monopolists of the "kosher" business, and to owners of catering halls and country hotels.

When we call the Jewish miscellany a "community," we prove that the Jewish community, far from being born, has not yet even been conceived.

So-called Jewish communities in America are accumulations of organizations, societies and institutions, maintained by Jews to help their fellow Jews.

An organic community would be an integrated body of Jews associated to help themselves, including those who are in special need of help.

Organic community is the only technique that will stop the draining away of life from Diaspora Jewry.

Try to talk Judaism to an American Jew who asks, "What have I in common with a Moroccan or an Egyptian Jew?" and you meet a blank wall of incomprehension.

It is much wiser to have a chicken lay eggs than to try to crowd it back into its own egg.

By the same token it is wiser to have the Synagogue keep on producing new forces and agencies in Jewish life than to try to crowd them back into the Synagogue.

Organic Jewish Community is a human problem, and human problems cannot be solved by theorizing about them. They can be solved only in action. (*Solvitur operando*.)

❖ ❖

The problem of Judaism cannot be solved by the Synagogue, because the Synagogue itself has become a problem.

❖ ❖

Jewish organizations which specialize in defense are about as Jewish as the much advertised Jewish rye bread.

5. *Anti-Semitism*

Anti-Semitism is the Jewish weather—the first topic of conversation among Jews and the last thing they can do anything about.

❖ ❖

The biblical prophets never foresaw that their writings would be read by non-Jews; else they would not have been so free with their denunciations of the Jews.

❖ ❖

Hate-mongers are a far greater menace to society than Typhoid Marys.

❖ ❖

There are some Christians whose sole claim to Christianity is their hatred of Jews.

There are some Jews whose sole claim to Judaism is their being hated by Christians.

❖ ❖

Must we Jews depend upon the fires of persecution to weld us into a people?

❖ ❖

Anti-Semitism is a disease to which even Jews are not immune.

The theory that anti-Semitism is the dislike of the unlike sounds right, but it is unsound.

On that theory, all husbands ought to dislike their wives.

The truth is that anti-Semitism is, in large part, Gentile isolationism resentful of the attempt of Jews to pass off as Gentiles.

To keep the freedom we Jews have, we should demand as much as we are entitled to by our inalienable rights. That calls for self-emancipation.

Jews who have no authentic knowledge about their own people are bound to accept as truth that image of their people which is refracted by the hates and prejudices of the bigots.

To expect anti-Semitism to subside if only Jews were more ethical than their neighbors, is like expecting a bull to refrain from chasing a vegetarian.

During World War II editors of large newspapers displayed a vulture-like discrimination in their choice of horror stories.

According to R. A. Davies, author of *Odyssey Through Hell*, editors cabled European reporters, "Our readers are tired of horror stories. Cable only if death rolls are unusually large or deaths unusually gruesome."

Stories about Jews, however, even when the deaths were numerous and gruesome, were rejected.

The reporter would receive word saying, "Atrocities against Jews not acceptable news material."

When Rudolph Hess was convicted of four million killings, the New York *Times* reported the verdict briefly on page eleven.

According to a study made some time ago, Germans of Protestant background tended to be more prejudiced (against Jews) than Catholics. In both groups, those who attended church regularly were more prone to anti-Semitism than those who did not.

It is quite evident that the so-called "Judeo-Christian emphasis on brotherhood" is not evenly distributed.

Most of the weight seems to rest on the Jewish leg.

The Christian leg has a terrible limp, if we are to judge from the study quoted above.

We invite the doctors of the *National Conference of Christians and Jews* to cure the sick leg.

Whatever makes our neighbors "Jew-conscious" makes us Jews self-conscious.

Why the two or three Jews who are admitted into an exclusive club, neighborhood, or school generally turn out to be *Judenfresser,* may be explained by the following parable of Pestalozzi's known as "Fishes and Pike."

The fishes in a pond brought an accusation against the pike who were making ravages against them.

The judge, an old pike, examined the charges and determined that the complaint was well-founded, and the pike were guilty. To make amends, therefore, the defendants were required to allow two ordinary fish every year to become pike.

"Anti-Semitism is the socialism of the fool," said the famous socialist August Bebel. Unfortunately, socialism is not fool-proof.

❖ ❖

The Jewish escapist's version of Judaism is that the fear of anti-Semitism is the beginning of wisdom.

❖ ❖

The Jew who hates himself for being a Jew and who finally succeeds in losing himself in Gentile society is merely a variant of the cannibal described by the anthropologist Margaret Mead in her book, *Male and Female.*

"When a Mundugumour became so angry that his anger turned against himself," she writes, "he got into a canoe and drifted down the river to be eaten by the next tribe."

❖ ❖

The play, *Edward, My Son,* has as its main character a Lord Holt, a man who rose from poverty to great wealth and a place in the English nobility by dint of a devious career, which began with arson. His inordinate ambition was spurred on by a possessive love for his son, whom his indulgence helped to make into a rake and a wastrel.

There is not the remotest possibility that Lord Holt will become an English stereotype that might incite riots or pogroms against Englishmen anywhere in the world.

Such is the luck of the English. When Shakespeare, however, portrays Shylock, a kind of Jew who never lived on land or sea, and pictures him driven by ceaseless baiting and the theft of his daughter Jessica to seek revenge, that Jew becomes a stereotype of avarice and hatred and is invoked as a reason for hounding his people.

Such is the *schlimmazel* (bad luck) of the Jews.

❖ ❖

"There were Jews, particularly in the upper economic levels," said Sherwood in his *Roosevelt and Hopkins,* "who supported the America First Committee, because their fear of anti-Semitism in America far transcended their resentment of Nazi barbarism in Europe; and there were some Jews who were just as ready as anyone else to 'do business with Hitler.'"

Perhaps our wealthy American Jews will learn once and for all, that by placing their personal interests above those of the Jewish people, they actually render a disservice to America and betray the cause of democracy.

❖ ❖

When legal pundits obstruct the enactment of laws designed to prevent the incitement to mass hatred and pogroms, they confirm the truth of the following by Oscar Wilde:

"There is only one thing worse than injustice, and that is justice without her sword in her hand."

❖ ❖

It is far easier to remove mountains than prejudice.

❖ ❖

Every Jew is, in some sense, a liability as well as an asset to his fellow Jews.

He is a liability because the anti-Semite can use him as an excuse to harass and persecute Jews in general. If he is a failure and a burden on society, other Jews are held responsible. If he is successful or achieves distinction he arouses the envy of his competitors, who take it out on his fellow-Jews.

❖ ❖

When a Jew who is ignorant of his people's tradition says he is proud to be a Jew, he displays neurotic pride.

Karen Horney defines neurotic pride as an "exalted self-esteem that is not built upon existing assets but upon imaginary superiority."

She goes on to say that "the more a person's whole being comes to rest on such pride, the more vulnerable he is. He feels then easily humiliated and reacts to it with vindictive impulses."

That explains why preoccupation with anti-Semitism is the obsession of Jews who are such in name only.

The moral problem of society, according to William James, is to find a moral substitute for war.

The spiritual problem of the Jewish People is to find a spiritual substitute for the defensive war against anti-Semitism as a basis for Jewish unity.

There are three types of organized efforts to fight anti-Semitism: one is to prevent it from stopping Jews who wish to cease being Jews, another is to prevent it from stopping Jews who wish to live as Jews, and a third is to increase the membership of some Jewish organizations.

In any oppressed minority there are always some who share the majority prejudices against their own kind.

The wolf in Aesop's fable blamed the lamb for muddying his stream, though the lamb was paddling far below him, and for having slandered him the year before, though the lamb wasn't even a year old. Would he have been persuaded by the National Conference of Christians and Jews to look elsewhere for his dinner?

The Christians held us responsible for the crucifixion of Jesus, and called us "Christ killers."

That kind of thinking is a hangover from an ancient and seemingly incorrigible habit of mind—that of holding an entire people forever responsible for some presumable misdeed of its ancestors.

Nachmanides ascribed the sufferings of our people at the hands of Moslems to Sarah's ill-treatment of Hagar, the mother of Ishmael, who was assumed to be the ancestor of the Arabs.

6. *Jews are like That*

Our sages were shocked to think that a time would come when Jewish children would be so ignorant of Judaism that they would wonder why their parents observed Pesah.

How would these sages have felt had they been able to foresee a time like ours, when Jewish children are so ignorant of Judaism that they wonder why their parents don't observe Easter, like everybody else?

American Jewish life would be much better off with federations of faith and hope than with federations of charity.

Many a rabbi deems it necessary to compromise with his convictions, on the assumption that "the beginning of wisdom is the fear" of the die-hards in his congregation.

There are Jews, who, like the novelist Elmer Rice, deem it a point of honor to call themselves Jews merely "because there are people who persecute Jews."

Why be Jews by the disgrace of man, when we can be Jews by the grace of God?

❖ ❖

Assimilationist Jews would like to turn all Jewish community centers into non-sectarian ghettos, to serve as a *nachtasyl* for our people on their way to the haven of complete loss of Jewish identity.

❖ ❖

A keen observation is that of the great scholar and thinker, Harry A. Wolfson, to the effect that many a Jewish apostate finds it easier to lose the relish for his father's God than for his mother's cooking.

❖ ❖

We Jews have been blessed with saints and with rationalists. We could stand, however, a few rationalist saints.

❖ ❖

The rabbis who had functioned as chaplains in the armed forces found it hard to resume their congregational routine.

The main reason was that, having had a taste of what it meant to be wanted, they found it hard going merely being needed.

❖ ❖

The romantic appeal which the traditional liturgy has for many Jews is largely due to the fondness which absence begets.

❖ ❖

Grass roots Hasidism did not become God-intoxicated the Buber way, through the contemplation of the "I-Thou" relationship.

They preferred the way of alcoholic *lehayyim*.

❖ ❖

Professor Sidney Hook tried to find out how many of his Jewish students would have wanted to be born Jews if they were given the chance to be born again.

What he learned is most disconcerting, "that the overwhelming majority of Jewish students did not want to be born again as Jews but as something else."

Why do Jews feel that way? Perhaps the answer is to be found in the following:

A Jew who had achieved financial success and had kept himself aloof from Jewish life was somehow drawn into Jewish activity. After a number of years during which his Jewish interests grew in scope and intensity, the question was put to him whether, if he were to be born again, he would choose to be a Jew.

His reply was: "If I were asked whether I would care to be born over again, I would certainly say, 'No.' But if I had to be born, and had to choose between being born a Jew and being born a non-Jew, I would choose to be born a Jew."

His answer makes clear that the reason for Jewish self-rejection is the kind of world we live in and that the prerequisite to Jewish self-acceptance is doing something for the Jews.

❖ ❖

Among the principal reasons for joining a synagogue nowadays are being in line for a seat for the holidays and celebrating there a son's bar mitzvah or a daughter's wedding.

❖ ❖

A new form of absentee landlordism is the recent increase in synagogue membership, accompanied by a decrease in synagogue attendance.

❖ ❖

It is not unusual these days to see a holy wreath hung on a *mezuzah* or to hear a Jewish woman ask the clerk at the toy store for a Hanukkah lamp which she promised to give her child for Christmas.

❖ ❖

What Max Brod has to say about Kafka applies to us Jews:

"Unable to accept the world, he turned himself into a universe. Of all believers he was the freest from all illusions, and among all those who see the world as it is, without illusions, he was the most unshakable believer."

To try to explain to the average American Jew the process of living in two civilizations is like trying to explain that the earth is round, to a man who says that it has always been flat where he lives.

Mankind is growing up. For some reason beyond our comprehension, we Jews have a larger share of the growing pains than the rest of mankind.

The High Holidays have come to be observed by many of our people as a kind of *yahrzeit* for the Judaism which died with their parents.

Jews whose only Jewish activity is attendance at High Holiday services should be designated as "revolving-door Jews."

They no sooner step inside Judaism than they step out of it.

There are three kinds of Jews.

There are the Jews who say with the Psalmist, "I shall not die but live."

There are Jews who are "tired of living and feared of dying."

And there are Jews who apologize for being "so unconscionably long a-dying."

There was a period in American Jewish life when Jews were Hebrews. Then they established Young Men's *Hebrew* Associations and Homes for Infirm *Hebrews!*

They knew then very little Hebrew. But they disliked the name "Jew."

Now Jews are Jews and all the better if they know Hebrew.

❖ ❖

On the train going to Chicago, I met a Jew, a man in the sixties, who was returning to his home in San Francisco from New York, where he had been for a reunion with a large family of brothers and sisters and their children.

He showed me a letter of profuse thanks which he had received from his rabbi, to whom he had sent as a gift a pair of *tefillin* he had himself written while still a *yeshivah bohur* in Russia.

Explaining his gift, he added, "No one in my entire family has any use for *tefillin;* so I gave them to my rabbi."

On the train from Chicago, I met a young Jew of eighteen who had landed in San Francisco three days before on his way from Shanghai to the Yeshivah of the Lubavitcher Rabbi in Brooklyn.

In Shanghai he had lived with his parents for the last eight years, and helped them to make a living by dealing in old clothes.

The last two years he devoted the greater part of his time to studying Talmud in the yeshivah there.

Now his ambition in life, as he naively put it, is to become a *"gadol ba-Torah,"* famous as a great scholar in the Torah.

When the time for *Maariv* came round, he went to the platform of the car and chanted his prayers so loud that he could be heard inside the car above the grinding of the wheels.

The contrast between the man and the youth made me think of the verse in *Kohelet* and the interpretation given it by the Rabbis:

"One generation goes, and another comes, while the earth endures perpetually."

" 'The earth' refers to Israel," said our sages.

❖ ❖

Our alienated Jewish intellectuals who write about Jewish life and Judaism would do well to remember the Chinese advice, that when you paint bamboo you must "become bamboo."

"Wie es sich christelt, so juedelt es sich" ("What Christians make of their Christianity, Jews make of their Judaism"), said Heine.

He said that in mockery. It happens to be an inevitable fact.

But though it is inevitable, it does not mean that Jews have to follow their neighbors blindly, nor that they have no choice in the matter.

It is also a fact that not all Christians make the same thing of their Christianity.

Some are retrogressive and irrationalist; others are progressive and rationalist.

These days thermostatically controlled oil or gas burners automatically furnish the right amount of heat; yet on cold days one sees log fires blazing brightly in the hearths, as in olden days before coal came into general use.

The two kinds of heat manage so to mingle as to render the atmosphere all the more comfortable and cozy.

Might not the homes of American Jews likewise be rendered all the more enchanting through the combined spiritual radiation of Israel's historical culture and America's highly modern civilization?

Jewish young people are required to make more renunciations than non-Jewish are. They should, therefore, be repaid with an extra measure of time, interest, companionship and love on the part of their parents and the Jewish community.

Formerly Jews would hire a "Shabbos-goy" to turn out the lights and make fire in the stove on the Sabbaths.

Now many congregations hire a rabbi to be their "Shabbos-Jew," to keep the Sabbath for them.

We Jews have less freedom to be Jews than we are entitled to. Nevertheless, we have more freedom to be Jews than we actually use.

The courage to be a Jew begins with the courage to bear a personal name that is outstandingly Jewish. (But we can take on American *family* names.)

There is every moral and psychological reason for taking the matter of Jewish names seriously.

What western civilization has contributed to stimulate creativity among Jews is best illustrated by the fact that they have been able, within a single century, to match a Goethe with a Heine, a Newton with an Einstein, a Darwin with a Freud, a Kant with a Bergson, and a Kierkegaard with a Buber.

We Jews have been the victims of man's cruelty over a longer stretch of time and to a far more intensive degree than any other people.

If *we* still have faith in Man, why should any one despair of him?

An interesting sidelight is thrown on the Jewish type of "foxhole" religion by an item in a report of the Jewish Welfare Board.

The number of Jewish men in the armed forces was about half a million.

The number of *mezuzahs* asked for by the Jewish soldiers was 1,300,000.

The number of pairs of *tefillin* was 4,500.

No two sayings reflect so accurately the contrast between the spiritual temper of the ancient Romans and the ancient Jews as the following:

The Roman saying is: *Discunt fata voluntem, nolentem trahunt* (The fates lead the willing and drag the unwilling).

The Jewish saying is: *B'derek she-adam rotze lelek molikim oto* (A man is led wherever he wishes to go).

Throughout its history, Judaism has been challenged and stimulated by non-Jewish philosophers. Ancient Alexandrian Judaism by Plato, medieval Judaism by Aristotle, modern German Judaism by Kant, contemporary American Judaism by John Dewey.

Jewish life in the past was poor in material resources, but rich in manpower. Today it is rich in material resources, but poor in manpower.

We realize with amazement how self-doubting our youngsters are, when so casual an expression as "Judeo-Christian tradition" is enough to bolster their self-confidence.

Once in a while rabbinical placement committees get a request like the following:

Please send us one of your graduates. He must be an A-1 orator, a good mixer, and it won't hurt if he doesn't look too Jewish.

Not to fit into any conventional category, not to be classifiable according to any established class system, not to be a stock size in religion, nationalism, or civilization—that is the price one has to pay for being a Jew.

❖ ❖

Time Magazine (Dec. 30/57) quoted Notre Dame's ex-president as challenging his fellow-Catholics to explain why it is that "for every 100,000 Jews in this country, there are 20 in *Who's Who* ... for every 100,000 Catholics, 7. ... Where are Catholic Salks, Oppenheimers, Einsteins?"

That a Catholic of such high standing should not know the answer is indeed amazing. If Salk and Oppenheimer and Einstein had their mentality shackled by the supernaturalism to which Catholics are committed, would they have been able to make their respective contributions to human knowledge?

❖ ❖

The modernized Jew resents the beggars at a funeral shaking the few coins in their charity boxes on which is inscribed the verse *Zedakah Tatzil Mi-mavet* (Zedakah saves from death). Then he goes home and sends in a contribution to some charity in memory of his departed friend.

Apparently it is not only substance that counts, but also form.

❖ ❖

The text, in Isaiah 60:21, does not read: "Thy people are *all-rightniks.*" It reads: "Thy people are *all righteous.*"

❖ ❖

The next luxury liner Israel builds for tourists will be called S. S. *Mein Kind* ("Eat, eat, my child").

❖ ❖

We wonder whether the gustatory image of the Jew created by Levy's rye bread, Hebrew National bologna, or bagel and lox will replace the theological image of the Jew as Christ killer, Judas Iscariot or as the Wandering Jew.

❖ ❖

IV. TORAH

1. *Tradition and Change*

Our present needs are determined by the past, which is beyond our control, and by the future, which is within our control.

❖ ❖

People who always find in the past what they miss in the present are generally unable to manage the future.

❖ ❖

To guide our lives by ancient traditions instead of by recently acquired knowledge is like trying to read by a candle light a thousand yards away, when we have an incandescent lamp overhead.

❖ ❖

Exaggerated traditionalism in politics, art, science or religion is a form of cultural thumb-sucking.

❖ ❖

It is far easier to precipitate change than to control it.

❖ ❖

It is easier to jump on the bandwagon than to get off it.

❖ ❖

Hypertrophy of power is mankind's most fatal ailment.

❖ ❖

Lord Acton's famous saying that all power corrupts is about as helpful as saying that all fire burns.

❖ ❖

Returning to some pre-modern universe of thought is possible for the modern man only in the same sense that it is possible to revisit the scenes of one's childhood.

People normally do that sort of thing only to satisfy a feeling of nostalgia, but not with a view of finding there a permanent home.

❖ ❖

The radical who is a fanatic about his *doxy* is no less given to ancestor worship than the Orthodox. The only difference is this: The Orthodox believes that his ancestors were wiser than he; the radical is sure that he is wiser than his descendants will be.

❖ ❖

A spiritual leader should not be merely a curator but also a creator of religion.

❖ ❖

Only a modern orientation can sustain our devotion to tradition.

❖ ❖

A Tennessee preacher is said to have smashed his time-piece when the Federal Government finally instituted the four zones of standard time.

Those who object to having changes in religious and ethical standards reflect changes in the conditions of life belong to the same tribe as that preacher.

❖ ❖

What is normative in an earlier era becomes descriptive in a later age.

❖ ❖

In the Great Society that is to be—if there is to be any Society at all—only a Greater Judaism will be capable of survival.

❖ ❖

No one, so far as we know, has discovered an effective serum for those who are allergic to new ideas.

❖ ❖

The monastery in the Middle Ages ministered less to ascetic devotion to God than it did to the regressive tendency of those who were too weak to face up to the harsh realities of the world.

The medievalists were convinced that they were intellectually and spiritually inferior to the ancients.

For once the medievalists were right.

Only a progressive is entitled to recite the benediction of *"Sheheheyanu."*

For the conclusion of the benediction reads *"Vehiggianu lazeman hazeh"* (He has caused us to reach this time), *i.e.,* "He has brought us up to date!"

Directing and acting are said to "make" the play.

Similarly, effective and relevant interpretation "makes" tradition.

Realizing that the authority of the past has lost its appeal, the reactionaries try the "new look" by claiming to be post-moderns.

The most difficult obstacle to surmount in any reform, whether political, economic or religious, is the popular assumption that once you get wet it doesn't make much difference how much wetter you get.

Every cloud has its silver lining. Likewise, the backwardness of vast numbers of human beings responsible for cultural lag has its compensations. They constitute a kind of "contemporary ancients," whom historians and anthropologists can study for the purpose of reconstructing the beginnings of civilization.

People who have a passionate desire to understand the mystery of death and evil are like children reaching for the moon.

Traditional theology babies such people; it leads them to believe that they can have the moon.

Modern theology should have the courage to persuade them to grow up.

It should make them realize that they should use their quickened sensitivity to misery and oppression, not to cogitate about them but to combat them.

❖ ❖

Traditional religion expected a saint to *perform* miracles; modern theology expects a saint to be a miracle.

❖ ❖

Nostalgia for an idealized past is a kind of *ersatz* piety, which is practiced by those who are too lazy, or too cowardly, to create a desirable future.

❖ ❖

For lack of fresh fuel we bank the fire with ashes to keep it burning.

For lack of new ideas we resort to outworn traditions to keep religion from being exhausted.

❖ ❖

The kind of religion that was adequate in the past is as inadequate for our spiritual needs as the little red school house is for our intellectual needs.

❖ ❖

It is much easier to unravel a tradition than to knit one.

❖ ❖

It is impossible to strengthen a limb which is kept tied down. It is likewise impossible to strengthen a religion which is held fast in a fixed set of rites and beliefs.

❖ ❖

Most of what passes for belief in God is really belief in our grandfathers.

❖ ❖

The future of man as a free spiritual being cannot be divorced from his past endeavors to become one.

❖ ❖

Those who have nothing to look back to have nothing to look forward to.
A people without a tradition is a people without hope.

❖ ❖

In olden times men made progress the way they do when they row a boat with oars. They moved forward with their faces to the receding past.
Nowadays they have to make progress the way they do when they drive a motor boat, with their faces to the oncoming future.
Difference in speed calls for a difference in the direction we face.

❖ ❖

At first men struggle to be free from nature; that gives rise to tradition. Then men struggle to be free from tradition, to get back to nature.

❖ ❖

If human beings made it a point not to draw inspiration from memories that are fictitious, they would not cherish hopes that are illusions.

❖ ❖

So long as the yardstick by which we measure human progress changes, it will be impossible to tell whether man makes any progress.

❖ ❖

We are bound to experience disillusion if we take literally the glamorous prophecies of our future, just as we are bound to suffer disappointment if we take literally the glowing description of our past.

❖ ❖

When you judge the future entirely by the past, what you lack may be called either faith or imagination.

❖ ❖

There are three kinds of changes possible in human life: evolution, which is slow and haphazard; revolution, which is rapid and destructive; reconstruction, which is deliberate and constructive.

❖ ❖

It is true that the future is conditioned by the past, but many different futures can be built on the same past.

❖ ❖

Many a bygone movement owes the greater part of its glory and enchantment to the distance that separates us from it.

That is the case with Puritanism in Christianity, Ralph Barton Perry notwithstanding, and with Hasidism in Judaism, Martin Buber notwithstanding.

❖ ❖

A tradition can live only so long as it continues to change.

❖ ❖

Traditionalists often act as if tradition were God, and belief in God only incidental to belief in tradition.

❖ ❖

A modest way of asserting omniscience is to have tradition back up your opinion.

❖ ❖

The ideas and ideals which a tradition transmits constitute spiritual capital.

Belonging to the past, they are like currency of a country from which we have migrated.

If they are to be put into circulation, they have to be converted into the currency of the present-day world.

The process of conversion is known as interpretation or re-interpretation.

That process enables the spiritual energy stored in a tradition to continue operating in worlds far different from those in which it arose and grew.

Man lives not only by facts but also by meanings. The stars of the heavens are facts; the constellations of the Zodiac are meanings. Energy is a fact; the theory of relativity is a free creation of the imagination. The atom bomb is a fact; its use will determine its meaning.

Yesterday's heresy that has become today's orthodoxy is like yesterday's roast that has become today's hash.

There can be no real change of heart without a real change of mind.

Religious liberals are charged by the Neo-Orthodox with addressing men of today in the language of *yesterday* (the language of Locke and Rousseau).

What then do the Neo-Orthodox do?

They address men in the language of *yesteryear* (the language of St. Paul and St. Augustine).

Why is it that in the interest of the future we often glamorize the past at the expense of the present?

If the past were really as glamorous as it is often made out to be, why is the present—its offspring—so irredeemably bad?

❖ ❖

In the case of social and religious practices that have outlived their usefulness, the law of diminishing returns becomes the law of self-defeating returns.

As Tennyson well put it:
"God fulfills Himself in many ways,
Lest one good custom should corrupt the world."

❖ ❖

When automobiles first came into use, many of them would stall in the middle of the road.

Mischievous youngsters, in malicious joy, would chorus: "Git a horse, git a horse."

That is the way many traditionalists act when the machinery of modernism stalls.

❖ ❖

The main hindrance to the development of Jewish law has been the assumption that to meet changed conditions, nothing more is necessary than to reinterpret the traditional law in such a way as to render it compatible with those conditions.

That assumption is not confined to Jewish law. Samuel Gompers is credited with the statement that "a precedent can almost always be found for a new idea, however revolutionary it may seem, if you really search for it."

The case of *prosbul,* a legal device for circumventing the biblical law that required the remission of all loans every seventh year, has always been held up as proof of the possibility of adapting Jewish traditional law to newer needs.

❖ ❖

Our traditionalists act like the man who, having once found a dollar in the gutter, always thereafter walked with his eyes glued to the ground, in hopes of finding more.

❖ ❖

The principle, "Make a fence about the Torah," tried to prevent transgressing the written law by adding to it unwritten prohibitions.

Modern experience, however, has shown that the multitude of unwritten prohibitions has contributed to the transgression even of the written ones.

The ancient authorities are entitled to a vote—but not to a veto.

To be contemporary does not necessarily mean being temporary.

If longevity were evidence of intrinsic worth, elephants should be of greater worth than humans.

If the age of a religious practice were a measure of its sanctity, the prayers that a Brahmin recites three times a day would be the most sacred of all prayers, since they consist of the same Vedic verses that were used as prayers three thousand years ago.

The conservative character of the popular mind and its resistance to change are exemplified in our continuing to call the *Amidah* (the part of the liturgy which is recited standing) *Shemoneh Esreh, i.e.,* Eighteen Benedictions, although it is more than eighteen centuries since a nineteenth benediction was added to it.

There comes a time when such lack of mental flexibility is fatal to a people. Our own day threatens to be such a time for the Jewish people.

Some rabbis preach as though nothing has happened since the days of the Talmud. Others preach as though nothing happened before the last Sabbath.

The doctrine of "Catholic Israel" is based on the recognition that change is inevitable and on the fear of taking a hand in it.

It is a form of faith in the unconscious wisdom of the species and of dread of the conscious intelligence of the individual.

❖ ❖

We should feel toward our tradition as we should feel toward our country:

My tradition right or wrong: if right, to be kept right; if wrong, to be set right.

❖ ❖

The cure for anxiety about the future is not nostalgia for the past.

❖ ❖

Those who assume that it is possible for new Jewish law to be enacted within the frame of traditional Jewish law often point to the Federal Constitution, as an illustration of a code that is made applicable to varying circumstances by means of interpretation.

They forget, however, that the Federal Constitution has been able to function in that capacity for two reasons:

First, because it is *inherently* subject to amendment; and

Second, because of the attitude toward it formulated by the late President Roosevelt, who urged the responsibility "to perfect, to improve, to alter when necessary, but in all cases to go forward."

❖ ❖

Whenever we change our way of life, our way of life changes us.

❖ ❖

The Jewish legalists among us hold that it is possible to adapt traditional law to modern conditions without violating the letter of the law.

By using an electric razor, for example, it is possible to get around all the five prohibitions against shaving.

Which seems to mean that if we are clever enough to invent the right kind of gadget, there is no telling what "God-given law" we might not get around.

❖ ❖

If tradition is to be a means to our growing up, it has to be partly outgrown.

❖ ❖

The expert forest ranger in charge of forest conservation often has to explain to tourists that, when they see tree stumps in a national forest, they should not think he has been selling out the nation's birthright to robber barons. "That's what people think," said such a ranger, "who haven't learned that conservation today in some cases means cutting down trees, not just leaving them to rot in noble splendor."

Would that some of our conservationist rabbis and other spiritual leaders had the intelligence and courage to do likewise with the spiritual heritage entrusted to them, and not leave everything that came down from the past to "rot in noble splendor."

❖ ❖

According to Carl Jung, the 1950 Papal proclamation of the dogma of the Assumption of the Virgin was "historically and psychologically necessary because the mass of Roman Catholic women unconsciously demanded it, to give them a symbol of identification in heaven."

Our Conservative Jews, to say nothing of the Orthodox, on the other hand, refuse to permit a woman to be called up to the Bimah, as a symbol of identification on earth.

❖ ❖

Tradition should be built upon, not lived in.

A sense of tradition is different from a sense of archaeology. Archaeologists are people who live in the past even when they are detached from it. Traditionalists are people who are attached to the past even when they refuse to live in it.

We are living on the same planet as our forebears, but in a different world.

Those who do not know tradition use it as an argument against change.

It is necessary to be rooted in a tradition in order not only to to have something to live by, but also something to rebel against.

The reason second-generation revolutionaries seldom have the distinction and thrust of their fathers is that they have nothing to rebel against.

We shall keep on "putting the cart before the horse," long after horses and carts have disappeared.

Those to whom every inherited folly is holy are mainly to blame for there being so many to whom everything holy is folly.

A tradition should be interpreted as a reflection of the past, and as an anticipation of the future, if it is to have any relevance to the present.

The traditionalist assumes that only our distant ancestors had religious experience. All that we, their descendants, are supposed to do is to enjoy our ancestors' religious experience by proxy.

❖ ❖

Professional pride inhibits barbers from using safety razors to shave themselves. They even boast of not knowing how to handle such vulgar little instruments. and they speak with contempt of those of their profession who in their own homes resort to safety razors.

Which only goes to show that opposition to change is the occupational disease of every profession.

A map that is three hundred years old may be priceless as an antiquity, but is worthless to one who travels by car to the places recorded on it.

Tradition may be indispensable as an inspiration to the good life, but worthless as a guide in living of it. To have tradition function also as a guide, it should be brought up to date.

Tradition puts Judaism in fetters. It is not enough to remove the fetters; what Judaism needs is wings.

Post-modern religion, which the neo-supernaturalists claim to be fostering, is as untimely and irrelevant as is pre-modern religion.

The Jewish sages put it well when they advised that the Torah should always be contemporaneous with life, neither behind nor ahead of the times.

Sadducees, Karaites, Orthodox—common to the three of them is insistence on freezing Jewish tradition.

T. S. Eliot gave the word "tradition" a new meaning. It was no longer something to be passively inherited but something to be obtained by "great labor."

In our era of expanding consciousness, with new objects coming within range, it is a mistake to invent new names for them. Whenever possible the old names themselves should be expanded so as to include them, together with the old and familiar objects. Only thus can we experience a sense of continuity and identity with the consciousness of our ancestors. Only thus can we have human history.

2. Biblical Interpretation

An excellent clue to the understanding of the Bible is to realize that it is the product of the endeavor by Israel's sages, priests and prophets to *re-educate their people*. They sought to eradicate misconceptions about life, God, man and the world, and to put in their place new conceptions.

The Bible is the first, and so far the only, evidence that a people can re-educate itself. Maybe that fact should constitute its main claim to being divine.

❖ ❖

It is much more difficult to interpret an event than to interpret a text.

When we interpret a text, we try to figure out what its author thought.

When we interpret an event we venture to figure out what God thinks.

❖ ❖

Nietzsche misread human character. He reviled the common man. He has been paid in kind. Few thinkers have been as misread as Nietzsche, and few have had so many curses heaped on their heads.

The German jingoists, for whom he had even greater contempt than for the common man, hailed him as their prophet, because they thought that he glorified war.

The truth is that the war he glorified was the war of ideas.

"If ye cannot be saints of knowledge," he says in *Thus Spake Zarathustra,* "then I pray you, be at least its warriors. . . . Your war shall ye wage for the sake of your thoughts."

His main interest is in the struggle with one's own passions and impulses for the sake of self-mastery.

That also happens to be the sense in which our tradition has taught us Jews to read the 27th Psalm, which is a song of Thanksgiving to God for rescuing us from the enemies that encamp against us.

These enemies are taken to be the demonic forces within us that threaten our moral and spiritual integrity.

That is the reason the 27th Psalm has been selected for daily reading during the penitential season.

❖ ❖

The most powerful anti-atom bomb weapon is the vast amount of misery human beings are capable of enduring when their spirit is aroused.

Thus the Bible proves to be right after all when it says: "Not by force shall man prevail."

❖ ❖

A dash of skepticism adds a welcome tang to the most solemn doctrine.

Even the Bible avails itself of it once in a while.

Preachers have come to be looked upon as jugglers who use the Bible as a kind of hat, out of which they pull rabbits in the form of moral lessons.

When, therefore, a preacher doesn't juggle texts, but unfolds their simple meaning and infers from them what their inherent logic implies, people don't believe their ears.

They say, "He is not a preacher; and what he says is not a sermon, but plain common sense!"

❖ ❖

A number of Psalms reflect a definite class struggle between the ungodly rich and the pious poor (cf. Psalms 10:3-4).

According to the Psalmist's theory of class conflict, godlessness is the opiate of the rich.

❖ ❖

There are nowadays two attitudes toward ambiguity in high places of religion and politics: the permissive and the prohibitive.

The permissive calls ambiguity "diplomacy"; the prohibitive calls it "double talk."

The prohibition of double-talk is clearly implied in the precept of the Torah, which forbids even the keeping of double-measures or double standards, to say nothing of using them (cf. Deut. 25:13-15).

❖ ❖

The difference between our Torah and other ancient and modern law codes is that the chief aim of those law codes is to establish law and order in society, whereas the chief aim of the Torah is to enable man to become fully human.

❖ ❖

According to *Ecclesiastes*, the people who wet their fingers all the time to see which way the wind blows never do much sowing.

❖ ❖

The Book of *Job* is a story of punishment in search of a crime.

❖ ❖

That things have to get much worse before they can get better is an ancient religious intuition expressed by the prophet Amos in the concept of the Day of the Lord.

❖ ❖

What could be more boring than complete knowledge?

Why then should we ascribe it to God, who, according to the Book of *Proverbs,* is being entertained by Wisdom? (cf. Proverbs 8:30).

❖ ❖

St. Francis preached to the birds.

According to Job, the birds preach to us (Job 12:7).

Christian theologians base man's need for a divine mediator to atone for his sins upon a very odd kind of reasoning.

Since God is infinite, man, who sins against God, is infinitely guilty: He therefore needs an infinite mediator to render infinite reparation for his sins.

That sounds as rational as charging a child with treason for innocently blurting out some state secret to an enemy.

The Psalmist who never studied philosophy or theology was apparently the wiser for it, as when he wrote: "God knows our frame; he remembers we are dust."

According to Spinoza, we learn from what Paul says about Peter more about Paul than about Peter.

Consequently, we learn from theology more about the theologians than we do about God.

In the Book of *Job* we encounter the first protest on record against the universal tendency to equate old age with wisdom (cf. Job 32:7).

❖ ❖

Like so many other things in the Bible, the scapegoat is not at all what people think it is.

They apply the term "scapegoat" to any person or group that is falsely charged with being the cause of the evils that befall them.

No one ever thought of holding the goat responsible for the sins it carried to Azazel.

The meaning of that ritual was that you had to get rid of evil before you tried to do good.

The wells that Isaac dug were stopped up by the Philistines.

Our sages interpreted that story allegorically. They said that the five wells Isaac dug symbolize the five books of the Torah, which are the waters of life.

That explains why anyone who stops up the wells of inspiration is called a philistine. He is usually an obstructionist on general principles.

The aggregate mind is less human than the solitary mind.

This should enable us to get the main point in the story of the revelation at Mt. Sinai.

The Ten Words, we are told, were uttered by God in the hearing of the entire people of Israel. That is because the people as a whole, no less than the individual human being, was expected to become morally responsible and spiritually mature. This explains why the entire people was addressed in the second person singular.

The author of the verse which represents God as having said of human beings: "I am sorry that I ever made them" (cf. Genesis 6:6), was the first Existentialist.

When Thoreau was on his death bed, someone asked him whether he had made his peace with God.

"I am not aware that I ever quarreled with Him," he replied.

That is the difference between him and Jeremiah, who did quarrel with God (cf. Jeremiah 12:1).

When a Christian holds forth on the principle of "turning the other cheek" as marking an advance over Jewish ethics, and a Jew retorts that the Jewish religion is too practical to embody such an impossible ideal, neither remembers that the principle of turning the other cheek was a Jewish doctrine several hundreds of years before the New Testament. It is stressed in the *Book of Lamentations,* Chap. 3:27-30, where we read the following: "It is good for a man that he should bear the yoke in his youth . . . Let him offer his cheek to the smiter, let him be sated with disgrace."

❖ ❖

To interpret the Torah properly, we must remember that the whole of it is more than the sum of its parts.

❖ ❖

The nearest the Bible comes to having a musical comedy, is the case of Jonah singing a psalm in the belly of the whale, and the whale not being able to endure him!

❖ ❖

A sympathetic interpretation of the miracle stories in the Bible is to treat them not as a record of physical but of psychological miracles, that is, of "abiding astonishment" at events that were intrinsically natural.

But we now need another psychological miracle to get people to appreciate the significance of "abiding astonishment."

❖ ❖

Moral delinquency of the Romans drew from Juvenal the same kind of invective and satire as that of the Jews drew from Isaiah.

But Isaiah spoke as God's messenger, and the Jews treated his written words as *sacred scripture.*

That points to the essential difference between Roman religion and Jewish religion.

❖ ❖

The Jewish philosopher Philo was the first to apply the allegorical method to the interpretation of the Bible.

According to him, Sarah, the wife of Abraham, symbolizes philosophy; and Hagar, the handmaid of Sarah, symbolizes the liberal arts, namely, grammar, geometry, music and rhetoric.

If Mother Sarah had a "sitter" for Isaac, the sitter probably would have symbolized the religious school.

❖ ❖

Rabbi Akiba taught:

"God so loved man that He made him in His own image."

"God so loved Israel that He gave them the Torah."

About the same time John of the Gospels wrote:

"God so loved the world that He gave up His only son, so that every one who believes in him may have eternal life, instead of perishing."

So far all that we Jews know of John's idea of God is: Christendom's practice not of God's love but of man's hate.

❖ ❖

The account of the fall of man, in the opening story of *Genesis,* is the ancient way of reminding us that man is only *on the way* to becoming human.

❖ ❖

The traditional warning against divulging the deeper meanings of scripture, to those who are not adequately equipped, should have been accompanied by a warning against the danger of having only a few adequately equipped.

❖ ❖

"Falling out of love with parents is the first step toward falling in love with a mate and beginning a new family."—John Levy and Ruth Monroe in *The Happy Family.*

That is said much better in *Genesis*:

"Hence a man leaves his father and his mother, and cleaves unto his wife so that they become one flesh."—Genesis 2:24.

❖ ❖

The way Joseph's brothers interpreted his night dreams, in which he beheld the sun, moon and stars paying him homage, as reflecting day dreams, is a psycho-analytic gem.

❖ ❖

The author of the prologue to the Book of *Job*, who apparently is not the author of the rest of the book, represents God as having permitted Satan to torment Job in order to prove to Satan that Job's piety has no ulterior motive.

Question: Did the author of the prologue mean to preach or to blaspheme?

❖ ❖

The Book of *Job* was evidently written by one who did not like theologians. He got even with them by writing a travesty on them. He added to Job's woes by inflicting on him four theologian friends, who bored and infuriated him with their arguments.

Fortunately, God himself told them off in time; otherwise Job would have lost his mind as well as his children, his health and his possessions.

❖ ❖

"Even the stork in heaven knows her time," says the prophet Jeremiah, "and the turtledove, swallow and crane keep the time of their coming; but my people know not the ordinance of the Lord."—Jeremiah 8:7.

Jeremiah thus assumed that the ordinance of the Lord, with its high principles of human conduct, is as natural as those that impel the birds in their migrations to observe the changes of the seasons.

That is a fallacy into which many religious thinkers have blundered.

The high principles of human conduct are natural only in the sense that they are *rational* and ought therefore to be lived up to.

Man's freedom to choose between observing and not observing them is both his opportunity and his peril.

The Bible is the most widely unread best seller.

To understand God is defined by Jeremiah, not as being able to account for the evil of sin and suffering, but as realizing that God exercises mercy and justice (cf. Jeremiah 22:23).

In the matter of modern biblical research, the Orthodox deny its premises, the Conservatives accept the premises but refuse to draw any conclusions, and the Reformers, for the most part, draw the wrong conclusions.

To prove that there are times when the laws of the Torah may be suspended or set aside, the Rabbis of old resorted to a verse, which, taken literally, says the very opposite.

The verse (Ps. 119:126) reads: "It is time for the Lord to act, for Thy law has been broken."

They interpreted that verse as saying:

When it is time to act for the Lord, men should break the law!

Which shows how the Bible has been used to prove whatever those who interpreted it wanted it to prove.

And which accounts for the fact that to use the Bible as authority for any policy of action is suspect.

We seldom realize that the first distinctive command issued to mankind by God, according to the Bible, is: master the world.

It is impossible to master the world without understanding it.

Science, which is an attempt to understand the world, and technology, which is an attempt to master it, are thus divinely ordained pursuits, *provided they are carried on as such.*

One of the cardinal sins of mankind is converting tools into idols (cf. Habakkuk 1:16).

Jewish tradition consists of the Written Torah, together with the interpretation given it by the Jewish folk spirit. That interpretation constitutes the Oral Torah.

In what way does the interpretation given by the Jewish folk spirit differ from that given by an individual commentator who does not embody that spirit?

The difference can be explained by what a music critic once said about the playing of a Rachmaninoff.

"When an average performer," he said, "sits down before the piano, he becomes smaller and smaller and the instrument becomes larger and larger."

"When a performer of the class of Rachmaninoff sits down to play, suddenly the piano begins to diminish and fades into a miniature, until finally it seems to disappear altogether—and you are left alone with the man and the music."

The Written Torah is the piano; the Jewish folk spirit is the performer.

When those who incarnate the Jewish folk spirit interpret the Written Torah, the latter fades into a miniature, and you are left alone with the Jewish folk spirit and the Divine music.

The famous physicist, J. Robert Oppenheimer, referring to the invention of the atomic bomb, said: "In some sort of crude sense the physicists have known sin, and this is a knowledge which they cannot lose."

When the Nobel prize winner and Oppenheimer's old Harvard teacher, Percy Bridgman, was told what Oppenheimer had said, he retorted, "If anybody should feel guilty, it's God. He put the facts there."

Bridgman thus proved the truth of the proverb:

"A man's own folly perverts his course; then he rages against God" (Proverbs 19:3).

❖ ❖

The foremost problem in Jewish religion is how to get Jews to take the Bible seriously without taking it literally.

❖ ❖

"It is common knowledge that speeches from the throne are written by Ministers."

If the Prime Minister read it, it would lack the symbolic significance of imperial unity which only the Queen's reading could give it.

Had Moses' name been appended to the Ten Commandments, they would have lacked the authority which only the name of God could give them.

❖ ❖

It is a sign of childishness to accept the great religious myths as literal truths, a sign of adolescence to regard them as delusion, and a sign of maturity to appreciate their spiritual implications.

❖ ❖

"To each one according to his needs," is not original with the Communists.

It is found in the Book of *Proverbs,* where we read: "Give me neither riches nor poverty: —provide me with food sufficient for my needs" (Proverbs 30:8).

❖ ❖

Although Adam's serpent is said to have been more clever than all the other beasts, he talked far less sense than Balaam's ass.

❖ ❖

It is not true that Einstein was the first to arrive at the formula that led to the making of the atomic bomb.

His formula led to the discovery of nuclear energy, with untold benefits for humanity.

The formula that led to the discovery of the atomic bomb was first discovered by Cain. He formulated it as a question: "Am I my brother's keeper?"

❖ ❖

"It is better to be a live dog than a dead lion," said Kohelet. But not an underdog.

❖ ❖

We find it difficult to understand why God should have forbidden man to eat of the fruit which could endow man with the knowledge of good and evil.

But Margaret Mead writes, "We have certainly not reached a stage in social awareness when ordinary functioning men and women can afford to carry about with them a knowledge of the cultural psychodynamics that unite them with the psychopath and the criminal."

❖ ❖

Some read nature from the standpoint of the Bible.

Others read the Bible from the standpoint of nature.

Most people, however, read the Bible and nature each from its own standpoint, and aren't in the least troubled by the difference in their standpoints.

❖ ❖

3. Jewish Practice

Alongside the vexing problem which agitates many an American Jew, whether or not to remain a Jew, the problem of ritual observance sounds like the problem of the split infinitive alongside that of the split personality.

❖ ❖

The rabbi was about to begin the wedding ceremony, when he noticed a man with a camera prowling nearby.

"Don't take any pictures," the rabbi warned sternly.

"Why not? That's my job. The only ones who object are the Catholics. Why do you insist on acting like Goyim?"

❖ ❖

Most people turn up their noses at a religious ceremony which lacks the patina of antiquity. Which only shows that to most people patina counts for more than what it covers.

❖ ❖

Meaningless rites remind one of burnt-out electric bulbs.

❖ ❖

To try to find in ancient Rabbinic law directions for ritual practice in our day is like hunting nowadays for the Northwest Passage.

❖ ❖

In the arsenal of theological anti-Semitism, a favorite argument is that Jews are given to legalistic pettifogging in their religion.

The truth is that this is a universal trait in religion.

Here is a sample in Christianity: In *Of Human Bondage* there is a scene in which Mary Ann put little Philip on the big family Bible so that he could reach the table.

His aunt cried out, "Oh, William, he can't sit on the Bible!"

❖ ❖

His uncle solved the difficulty by interposing the prayer book between Philip's small breeches and the Bible.

❖ ❖

"So high is the status of repentant sinners (*baale t'shuvah*) that not even the confirmed saints (*tzadikim gemurim*) can reach it."

What greater compliment could Jews "to the manner born" pay to "self-made" Jews?

❖ ❖

"The twist is the same—but the taste is different," the motto used in advertising pretzels with butter, might as well serve for a reinterpreted rite.

❖ ❖

Jewish scholars who draw from their scholarship no practical conclusions for Jewish life, are like a man who builds a castle but lives next door in a shanty.

❖ ❖

How solvent an effect the environment has on one's Judaism depends upon how soluble one's Judaism is.

❖ ❖

The legalistic spirit is as much out of place in ritual observance as is awareness of rules of elocution while delivering a speech.

❖ ❖

The past should live in the present as a memory and not as a ghost.

❖ ❖

What hypocrites nostalgia makes of us all!

❖ ❖

Reaction, even in retreat, puts up enough of a fight to bring about rear-guard success.

Such successes are often mistaken by those who have a limited view of the struggle as the final defeat of progress.

What Judaism needs is not a philosophy that can move men to tears but one that can move them to action.

❖ ❖

A religion without ritual is like a suit of clothes without buttons.

❖ ❖

They who confine their religion to the holidays give their religion a holiday the rest of the year.

❖ ❖

No religious ritual—however acceptable to the mind and the heart—can stir us unless accompanied by the rhythm of music, the dance, or the march.

❖ ❖

Our great prophets kept urging us to major in ethics and minor in ritual observances.

Those who reverse the order may develop the wrong sense of values shown by some of our people in pre-war Germany. They never missed the singing of *zemiros* on the Sabbath, but they sang some of them to the tune of *"Deutschland Uber Alles."*

Some of our fellow Jews in the South, who do not major in either ethics or in religious observance, think it necessary to outdo their fellow whites in their zeal for white supremacy.

❖ ❖

Ex-Orthodox Jews who are "either-or-nicks," and who say that if you are not an Orthodox Jew you are a make-believe Jew, sometimes ends up by becoming "go-the-whole-hog-nicks" and abandoning Judaism entirely.

❖ ❖

A second-day holiday is about as pleasurable as drying yourself with a wet towel.

❖ ❖

4. Jewish Education

With the de-Christianization of the western world, the Bible is coming to be regarded as a classic to be revered but not read.

With the establishment of the State of Israel, the Bible is beginning to be studied, even if not revered.

❖ ❖

If Hebrew is music to your ears, you are in love with the Jewish people.

❖ ❖

With Judaism as a three thousand year old civilization, the state of Jewish knowledge in this country may be described as one in which "never did so many know so little about so much."

❖ ❖

A Sunday School education is like seeking to know the world by reading a few Baedekers.

❖ ❖

Learning gives one power.

All the more remarkable, therefore, is it that among Jews the men of learning wanted to spread learning and were not worried that their own authority would suffer.

❖ ❖

Jews who refuse to study about Judaism but want to be convinced of its worth and greatness, are as reasonable as people who refuse to go into the water before they have learned to swim.

❖ ❖

The ambition of a Jewish child to acquire a Jewish education is bounded by the expectation of his parents, which is clear mainly on one point: they don't want him to become a rabbi.

❖ ❖

The study of Torah was not intended to provide a body of knowledge but rather a religious experience.

❖ ❖

The main reason so many of our people do not know what to be Jews *for* is that they have nothing to be Jews *with*.

❖ ❖

Sunday Schools, from the Orthodox and Conservative points of view, are a delusion educationally, but a potent snare with which to catch members.

❖ ❖

In Judaism the study of the Torah was a universal obligation. It was neither a leisure class privilege, as in the West, nor a ruling class requirement, as in the East.

This fact made the study of Torah unique as a means to human self-fulfillment or salvation. And this fact it is which should make everything that leads to self-fulfillment or salvation a part of the study of Torah.

❖ ❖

The artist Max Band was twitted by some of his friends for his enthusiasm over the Genizah fragments of the Library of the Jewish Theological Seminary.

(These are the fragments of ancient Jewish manuscripts, which have yielded up many a valuable literary treasure that had long been lost.)

What's so wonderful about a lot of ancient moldy scraps of parchment? He replied,

"That is the mold which yields penicillin, the penicillin Jews need to kill the dangerous bacteria of self-contempt."

❖ ❖

Speaking before the New England Council, Dr. James B. Conant once said: "If the leading citizens of this country would spend a tenth of the time and effort on vital problems of education that they spend on hospitals or the discussion of foreign policy, both highly commendable activities, I cannot help believing that the future of our democracy would be more secure."

For a sharp insight into Jewish life, substitute in Dr. Conant's statement, in strategic places, only the words "Jewish," "anti-Semitism," and "Jewish life!"

❖ ❖

The difference between a Hebraic Judaism and a non-Hebraic Judaism is like the difference between traveling through interesting country and looking at a movie travelogue of it.

❖ ❖

Without rootedness in Jewish life and a passion to maintain it, the response to a knowledge of its history and religion is likely to be, "So what?"

❖ ❖

To be self-sustaining, a people has to attend to its economy.

To be self-renewing, it has to attend to the education of its youth.

❖ ❖

Having a rooster in a coop back of the house and hearing him crow a few times a day, or a plaster mamma duck and four little baby ducks on the front lawn of a suburban home, can not substitute for the training children get on a farm from the care of cows, sheep and horses.

Neither can the two hour Sunday School curriculum substitute for the training which Jewish children receive in a Jewish environment.

❖ ❖

The trouble with present-day religious education is that it fails to teach people what they should expect of religion.

All it teaches at present is that religion means loyalty to one's particular denomination and traditions.

What it should teach is that religion should encourage freedom of thought, emphasize the service of man as the highest service of God, and insist on our regarding all human beings as deserving to be served.

So long as that kind of religious education is non-existent, the only kind that can succeed is the one that depends for its support either upon raffles or upon promises of pie in the sky.

A rabbi teaching an adult group was shocked when one of his students asked him whether Moses' second name was Maimonides.

Yet Mohammed managed to be the founder of a religion, even though he confused Miriam (Mary), the mother of Jesus, with Miriam, the sister of Moses.

Ancient peoples projected their favorite occupation into heaven. What the happy hunting grounds were for the American Indian, the *mesivta d'rakia,* or heavenly academy, was for the Jews.

Goethe's statement, that sentiment unites people while opinion divides them, should serve as a reminder that the main purpose of Jewish education should be to instil Jewish sentiment rather than to indoctrinate Jewish opinions.

The trouble with people who want to learn the whole Torah while standing on one foot is that they haven't a leg to stand on.

Techniques in education, whether it be Jewish or general, are like oxygen tents—useful only when there is oxygen.

Cicero the Roman started the idea that those who needed religion were mainly the ignorant.

The Jewish Sages taught that an ignorant person could not be truly religious.

❖ ❖

Jewish survival, like all other forms of human survival, depends upon progress in the creation of new words for thought and new tools for action.

❖ ❖

A multimillion dollar temple may galvanize Judaism, but an effective system of Jewish education will vitalize it.

❖ ❖

If the metamorphosis of man were accepted not merely as a verbal sentiment, but as an inevitable directive to becoming fully human, the main function of education would be teaching each successive generation how to negotiate the transition from the past of mankind to its future.

❖ ❖

The truth of Bacon's statement that knowledge is power is most dramatically demonstrated by the knowledge that vast energy is contained in matter and can be released by human intervention.

❖ ❖

If the purpose of education is to inculcate a sense of reality, it must make provision for enough courage not to run away from reality when it is actually sensed.

❖ ❖

The appetite for eating grows with eating.
The appetite for learning grows with learning.

Indoctrination is shoehorning the mind into tight situations.

❖ ❖

Seminary, etymologically, means "seedbed," not hothouse.

❖ ❖

The difference between education and indoctrination is that education is training for freedom, while indoctrination is training for obedience and conformity.

❖ ❖

The transformation of adult Jewish education into a concern with the total formation of man is a prerequisite for the transformation of Jewish society.

❖ ❖

The only Jewish scholars who can save the Jewish people from vanishing are not those with computer capacity, recording what was or what is, but with inventive capacity, proposing what can and ought to be.

5. *Family Relations*

Children are as little desirous of using their parents' mental furniture as they are of using their parents' dining-room furniture.

❖ ❖

Men's vanity makes their wives parasitic; women's envy makes their husbands avaricious.

❖ ❖

More important than knowing the statistics about the sex behavior of the human male on the animal level would be to know how to manage those ideas which raise the level of his sex behavior above that of the animal.

But that kind of information is not likely to make a "best seller."

If husband or wife were less eager to make each other over to please themselves, and more eager to make themselves over to please each other, the divorce rate would come down a good deal.

The problem of education, whether general or Jewish, is not that of problem children but mainly of problem parents.

When we reason with a child, we not only treat him as a person but we also help him to become one.

G. B. Shaw came from a turbulent home. His father was a heavy drinker, a poor provider and a bad husband.

This gave a decidedly puritan bent to Shaw's character; he turned out to be a teetotaler.

Children sometimes react against their home background for ill as well as for good.

Mysterious, indeed, are the ways of children with parents.

The ancients were full of advice to children and grandchildren.
The moderns are full of advice to parents and grandparents.

Parents do their children a great disservice if they fail to give them a religious training, and a far greater disservice if they give them the wrong kind of religious training.

The warmth of the home, even if at times rather suffocating, is more likely to hatch the basic human virtues than the free but humanly cold atmosphere of the hotel.

If we want to make sure that our children and children's children will accept and foster the Jewish heritage, we should amend the fifth commandment to read, "Honor your son and daughter that you may have a long life in the land which the Eternal your God is giving you."

V. RECONSTRUCTIONISM

To live as a Jew in the diaspora is like trying to walk up in a down-moving escalator. It is not easy, but with a little practice it can be done.

❖ ❖

Those who maintain that it is impossible for Jewish life to flourish anywhere but in Israel should be reminded that agronomists are inventing ways of raising crops in troughs.

❖ ❖

Thomas Huxley maintained that next to being right, the best thing is to be clearly and definitely wrong.

His theory was that, if you are so absolutely wrong, you are bound to have "the extreme good fortune of knocking your head against a fact, and that sets you all straight again."

That is why, next to being a Reconstructionist, the best thing for a Jew is to be uncompromisingly Orthodox.

❖ ❖

The Reconstructionist movement is, in a sense, trying to act the analyst to us Jews. The task is to have us grow up and learn to let go of Mamma Tradition's apron strings without rejecting Mamma altogether.

But as in *Deep Analysis* by Charles Berg, which describes in detail a single case of "analysis," the patient, after having undergone treatment for several months, comes to the analyst complaining: "I am fed up with it. I am fed up with you."

Analyst: "Then why come?"

Patient: "Well, I am not quite sure that I am really well enough."

Analyst: "Are you fed up with what I am doing to you, or are you fed up with what I am not doing to you?'

Patient: "I am fed up with what you are not doing. I feel I ought to ask you what I should do during the day. I want a course of discipline."

Analyst: "So you are not quite well enough."

One who expects Reconstructionism to provide a new hour-by-hour *Shulhan Arukh* is "really not quite well enough."

❖ ❖

Old castings which cannot be used in a new type of building do not have to be thrown away; they can be heated up and welded into new shapes.

Neither need we scrap traditional ideas and values which have become obsolete. If properly reinterpreted and reconstructed, they can serve very useful purposes in the new world we inhabit.

❖ ❖

The snide remark of certain journalists that "Reconstructionism makes the comfortable more comfortable" has as much truth to it as the opinion of Jewish anti-Semites that Judaism makes the miserable more miserable.

❖ ❖

The most revolutionary step in the reconstruction of our tradition was taken by our great Jewish historians, Marcus Jost, Graetz, Yitzhak Weiss, and Simon Dubnow.

If they had not secularized the story of the Jewish past by subjecting it to the laws of historical cause and effect, the Jewish people might have ceased to be a reality and would have evaporated into a myth.

❖ ❖

There were eminent **scientists with** aerodynamics at their fingertips who said that it was impossible to build an airplane heavier than air.

Along came a repair shop mechanic, who knew little, if anything, of aerodynamics, and built an airplane.

There are eminent sociologists and anthropologists, who are experts in human relations, who say that it is impossible for Jewish life to maintain itself in the diaspora.

Perhaps the Reconstructionists are the repair shop mechanics who can so build Jewish life that it will be able to maintain itself even in the diaspora.

❖ ❖

A people can live as long as it can reconstruct its life to meet changing conditions.

❖ ❖

Men say the future isn't what it used to be.

Neither is the past.

Both are in need of reconstruction if we are to have a livable present.

❖ ❖

Much of our traditional record of the past is myth, and much of our past is without record. That is why we are in need of reconstructing our past.

❖ ❖

Reconstructionism seeks to put gates through the fences that divide Jews into sects.

❖ ❖

Reconstructionism tries to say old things in a new way and new things in an old way.

❖ ❖

Reconstructionism, far from claiming to have said the last word concerning Judaism, religion, ethics or salvation, stresses the importance of saying the first correct word in each instance.

❖ ❖

The trouble with the Reconstructionist Movement is that it holds out no panaceas and no immediate solution, but only conditional promises and long range plans. That is its truth and distinction. It refuses to cater to wishful thinking. That is what its opponents describe as its "forbidding intellectual character."

Reconstructionism attempts to strengthen the fabric of Jewish life by attending to both its warp and its woof.

The warp that is in need of strengthening is the spiritual unity and status of the Jewish people.

The woof that is in need of mending is what gives Jewish life its manifold pattern of religion, ethics, culture.

In describing what makes human beings fully human, the philosopher R. B. Perry states: "They not only possess adaptation but acquire it. They exhibit not only organization and adaptation but reorganization and readaptation."

Reconstructionism is thus the application to the Jewish people of that which makes human beings fully human.

Traditional Judaism was sick:

Came the Orthodox doctors and prescribed more prayer and *mitzvot*.

Came the Reform doctors and advised the amputation of nationhood.

Came the Secularist doctors and advised the amputation of religion.

Came the Conservative doctors and said that all that traditional Judaism needed was a change of climate of opinion.

Came the Reconstructionist doctors and pointed out that what Judaism needed was neither prayer nor surgery, but mental therapy. It needed first to rid itself of delusions of grandeur that alternate with a sense of guilt and inferiority. And then it needed to acquire both a sense of reality and a faith in its own capacity to meet life on its own terms.

❖ ❖

The evolving theology of the Jewish religion is unique because it is the only theology that expresses the fears and hopes of a people, and not the cold cogitation of professional theologians.

❖ ❖

Many get on the bandwagon of Reconstructionism only to hitchhike to their own favorite destination—an excuse for being less Jewish.

❖ ❖

Reconstruction is more drastic than reform and less disturbing than revolution.

❖ ❖

Reconstructionism is intended to be a method of thought and organization of Jewish life, which can convert it from a liability to a reliability.

❖ ❖

Reconstructionism is at its best when it functions like the Socratic method of inquiry, in which the method and not the conclusion is the essential.

❖ ❖

Reconstructionism has its sidewalk superintendents who are fascinated by the machinery and the men at work in renovating the old House of Israel, but who wouldn't think of giving a helping hand.

❖ ❖

An illustration of what it means to live in three civilizations simultaneously is a sign in Miami, Florida, advertising "Kosher Hungarian Goulash in Dixie Style."

❖ ❖

The Orthodox conception of the ideal Jewish life is to swim against the stream.

The Reform view is that Jewish life can be lived by swimming with the stream.

The Reconstructionist view is that Jewish life is a matter of swimming across the stream.

Those who complain that Reconstructionism requires thought are like the man who complains bitterly that he has nothing to eat but food.

The three stages through which every new theory passes, according to William James, are: 1) its critics condemn it as absurd; 2) they dismiss it as trivial and obvious; and 3) they finally claim it as their own discovery. Reconstructionism is that kind of new theory.

The task of reconstruction is similar to the rebuilding of a railroad terminal while keeping the trains running. One must avoid waiting so long that the building collapses, yet build so skilfully that traffic may continue.

The difference between Judaism as a religion and Judaism as a civilization is the difference between a *point* of reference and a *frame* of reference.

Construct or reconstruct; don't merely conserve or reform.

The basic principle of theology in a new key is that to believe in God we have to believe in man.